HOW TO LEAD

The Second Edition of
Leadership *for* Learning

M J BROMLEY

Published by Spark Books UK

Spark
EDUCATION BOOKS

Published by Spark Education Books UK
Twitter: @SparkBooksUK

Published in 2018
© Matt Bromley 2018

The right of Matt Bromley to be identified as the author of this work has been asserted by him in accordance with the Copyrights, Designs and Patents Act 1988

This eBook is copyright material and must not be copied, reproduced, transferred, distributed, leased, licensed or publicly performed or used in any way except as specifically permitted in writing by the author or publishers, as allowed by the terms and conditions under which it was purchased or as strictly permitted by applicable copyright law.

ISBN-13: 978-1981361878
ISBN-10: 1981361871

CONTENTS

Introduction
1. What do school leaders do?
2. What qualities make a great school leader?
3. How can school leaders strike a work life balance?
4. Why do great school leaders need a vision?
5. Why does school improvement requires leaders not managers?
6. How can leaders transform a failing school?
7. What does it take to be a 'good' school?
8. What do 'outstanding' schools look like?
9. How can school leaders run a successful inspection?
10. How can school leaders manage change?
11. How can school leaders avoid common change management mistakes?
12. How can school leaders manage conflict?
13. How can school leaders manage teachers' performance?
14. What role can coaching and mentoring play in schools?
15. What does effective professional development look like in schools?
16. How can school leaders manage the business?
17. How can school leaders make effective use of Pupil Premium funding?
18. What does an effective exams analysis look like?
19. How can school leaders work productively with governors?
20. How can school leaders engage parents?
21. What does effective community cohesion look like?
22. What kind of school leader is the most successful?
23. What kind of school is the most successful?
24. How can school leaders recruit and retain good teachers?

INTRODUCTION

Why should you read this book?

Countless books have been written on the subject of school leadership: some claim to know the philosophy of school leadership; others promise to share the secret of school leadership. Many of these books have value; they contain nuggets of useful information based on detailed research. But most are theoretical; they are not practical. Once read, they are rarely again consulted. As good as they are, school leaders do not turn to them when they need ideas or inspiration.

I hope you regard *How to Lead: The second edition of Leadership for Learning* as something different; I hope you regard it as a practical handbook for busy senior leaders, a book of ideas which can be put into immediate practice and which can be dipped into when help and advice are needed most.

This author is different, too: I am not a university professor writing an academic research paper on leadership theory; I am an experienced senior leader who's worked in a range of schools and colleges - as well as in leadership roles in the private sector.

I have been an assistant headteacher, a deputy headteacher, and a headteacher. I have at one time or another managed every aspect of a school. I have managed the process of school improvement and self-evaluation, the curriculum and timetable, teaching, learning and assessment, pastoral care, administration, finance and the site.

I have helped schools and colleges on the journey towards 'outstanding': one school became a beacon of good practice in teaching and learning; another became the highest achieving comprehensive school in its authority and one of the top five most improved schools in the country, a school judged 'good with outstanding features' by Ofsted within three years of being in 'special measures'.

In my most recent full-time leadership role, as Group Director of a large FE college and multi-academy trust, the Ofsted judgment for further education provision improved from 'requires improvement' to 'good' with outstanding features, teacher training provision was graded 'outstanding', higher education provision was 'commended' by the QAA, and exam results placed the college within the top 20th percentile in the country. The secondary academy for which I was a sponsor and governor achieved the best GCSE results in its history.

*

Throughout my leadership career, I've seen examples of good and bad practice and have learnt valuable lessons from each. This book is a means of sharing my lessons in leadership…

A caveat: no book can teach you how to be an effective school leader. What's more, there is no philosophy and no singular secret to share.

The job of leading schools – as with leading any organisation – is far too complex and nuanced for that.

To begin with, each leader is different: each leader has a personality and style of his or her own which is the culmination of unique life and work experiences. Each school and each student is different and requires a personalised approach. Each situation, too, is different and requires a pinch of pragmatism and common sense, plus a generous helping of humanity.

In short: no problem is the same as the previous one and therefore no solution can be.

So *How to Lead: The second edition of Leadership for Learning* cannot tell you how to deal with every situation you encounter but it can provide you with the tools you need to construct your own leadership style and build an outstanding school.

In this book I will explore what is meant by effective leadership and what school leaders need to do to drive the school improvement process forwards.

CHAPTER ONE:
What do school leaders do?

What is school leadership?

School leadership – like all forms of leadership – is about setting direction. This is done by agreeing and articulating a shared vision, then by setting clear goals and performance targets that help bring that vision about.

The role of a school leader is often misunderstood and its scope underestimated by those outside the teaching profession. They remember the heads and deputy heads from their own childhoods as little more than the school's chief disciplinarians and the people who spoke soporifically in assemblies. But since the advent of grant-maintained status (following the Education Reform Act of 1988) school leaders have been much more than that: today, they are akin to the CEOs, finance directors and HR directors of medium-sized businesses all rolled into one (and this is not to mention their continuing role as chief disciplinarians and soporific speakers).

School leaders, therefore, have their fingers in many pies: they manage people; they manage projects; they manage processes; they manage information and communication; they manage finances, the site and health and safety; they develop and foster systems for monitoring, evaluating and reviewing performance; they manage governance; and they develop themselves and others - creating future leaders - using systems and processes wisely. This is a big job and if school leaders are to strike a healthy work-life balance (which they must if they are to survive their first term) they must not micro-manage each of these areas personally but must instead empower others - through artful School leadership – like all forms of leadership – is about setting direction. This is done by agreeing and articulating a shared vision, then by setting clear goals and performance targets that help bring that vision about.

The role of a school leader is often misunderstood and its scope underestimated by those outside the teaching profession. They remember the heads and deputy heads from their own childhoods as little more than the school's chief disciplinarians and the people who spoke soporifically in assemblies. But since the advent of grant-maintained status (following the Education Reform Act of 1988) and more recently with the introduction of academies and free schools which report directly to central government, school leaders have been much more than that: today, they are akin to the CEOs, finance directors and HR directors of medium-sized businesses all rolled into one (and this is not to mention their continuing role as chief disciplinarians and soporific speakers).

School leaders, therefore, have their fingers in many pies: they manage people; they manage projects; they manage processes; they manage information and communication; they manage finances, the site and health and safety; they develop and foster systems for monitoring, evaluating and reviewing performance; they manage governance; and they develop themselves and others - creating future leaders - using systems and processes wisely. This is a big job and if school leaders are to strike a healthy work-life balance (which they must if they are to survive their first term) they must not micro-manage each of these areas personally but must instead empower others - through artful delegation and through the creation of effective leadership structures - to be accountable.

Good school leaders, then, are about strategy and direction not day-to-day management. Good school leaders should concentrate on modelling the behaviours they expect from others (such as positivity and optimism, passion and determination). Good school leaders should develop people through support and understanding and should re-design their organisation (through a process of collaboration) in order to become - or continue to be - outstanding.

A good school leader is synonymous with being:
- a good listener; able to care about and respond to people's needs
- consistent, fair and honest; transparent and above reproach
- sensitive, able to show warmth and to empathise with people's concerns and worries
- able to give quality time to people, be available and approachable
- able to show assertiveness, determination and strength of response, yet be kind and calm and courageous
- able to communicate - through a variety of means and in an appropriate manner - with enthusiasm, passion and drive.

A good school leader should not and must not be consumed by what other people think. It is important that they are guided by their school's shared vision, and by their own determination and commitment to make a genuine and positive difference to young people's lives.

Moreover, a school's stakeholders - staff and governors, parents and students - will respond to a school leader who:
- is dynamic and forward thinking
- is sensitive to the needs of all and recognises hard work
- provides the necessary support others need
- trusts his/her staff and empowers them to make decisions and act on their own initiative
- does not place undue administrative burdens on his/her staff (i.e. keeps 'paper work' to a minimum and only calls meetings that serve a purpose)

*

There are many ways in which we could define and perhaps even measure the effectiveness of a school leader but I think it is reasonable and indeed practical to meld the myriad activities in which leaders are required to engage into six categories. These six realms of school leadership are as follows:

1. Setting a vision for the future
2. Being a lead teacher
3. Working with and developing others
4. Leading the organisation
5. Managing the team
6. Developing external links

Each school and each school leader will have a different interpretation of what the six realms mean to him or her in practice but here is my summary:

Setting a vision for the future

1. *Setting a vision for the future*

Setting a vision for the future is a key responsibility of any school leader because they need to have a vision for their school and need to articulate this clearly and with enthusiasm to stakeholders. School leaders need to know what sort of organisation they want their school to be and this should guide their decision-making. School leaders should take account of their school's local and national context, not only in terms of their vision but also in their everyday actions. They should think strategically and involve their stakeholders in their decisions. They need to show conviction of purpose: they must be driven by their vision and not be distracted by setbacks or conflicts.

Being the lead teacher

2. Being the lead teacher

Schools are seats of learning and so leading the teaching and learning agenda is a key role for senior leaders. Being the lead teacher is about having high expectations of all your teachers and about demanding the best for every student in your school. This means leading by example by continuing to be an excellent classroom practitioner who is able to engage and enthuse students, and by being up-to-date with the latest pedagogical thinking. This also means evaluating teaching and learning effectively – through a variety of means including lesson observations, learning walks, student voice, work sampling and the scrutiny of assessment records – and working with others to improve the quality of teaching and learning and to challenge underachievement (by working with data and investing in intervention and support).

Working with & developing others

3. Working with and developing others

School leaders need to foster a collaborative culture and provide learning opportunities for all their staff. They need to value the importance of continuing professional development through performance management and INSET. They should have high expectations of everyone in their school. School leaders should, again, lead by example and take their own professional development seriously. They should be well-informed and up-to-date with the latest educational thinking and research, as well as government policy (both central and local).

Leading the organisation

4. Leading the organisation

School leaders should share responsibility through effective delegation. They should demonstrate good judgment, be decisive but thoughtful, and should manage school resources effectively. They should manage their school's finances (although the day-to-day management of school finances should be delegated to a finance manager, this is one aspect of school leadership for which a headteacher/principal should retain responsibility; a headteacher/principal should fully understand the school finances and be accountable for fiscal decisions) in order to ensure their school achieves value for money. It is a school leader's duty to use public money wisely. This is achieved by being prudent, by planning ahead (including detailed costs in the school improvement plan) and by prioritising spending according to greatest need and according to the impact that spending will have on learning.

School leaders should also manage the site ensuring it complies with health and safety regulations and safeguarding. School leaders need to ensure that resources match the curriculum. Finally, senior leaders should manage the school's most important – and costly – resource: staff. This means ensuring that supply meets demand (in practice, this might involve restructuring) and that all staff have the tools and skills they need in order to do their jobs well (this means appropriate training but also evaluating whether staff have the requisite capability and, if not, taking appropriate action).

Leading the organisation is often a part of the job that school leaders find most challenging and difficult because they have trained as teachers not managers, but it is also the most important part of the job if a school is to move forwards and achieve sustainable improvements.

Managing the team

5. Managing the team

School leaders should take responsibility for their decisions and for the performance of their school. They should ensure clear accountability at all levels through effective line management structures and by drawing clear links between the school improvement plan and what is happening in school. They should analyse performance regularly and robustly, and give clear feedback and performance reports to stakeholders.

School leaders have legal accountability for what happens in their school as well as moral accountability. They should do what they think is right and should take advice from others – including their local authority and trade unions – wherever possible. But above all they should do what is right for their school and take decisions that will stand up to tough scrutiny over the long-term.

Developing external links

6. *Developing external links*

School leaders should develop and encourage effective partnerships with other schools, agencies and the community. Community cohesion is often misunderstood – or at least underestimated – as only referring to a school offering its site to the local community. Enabling community use is certainly important – be that by leasing your fields to the local football team or by running adult education classes in the evenings – but community cohesion is also about respecting diversity and protecting vulnerable students. It is about understanding the local community and taking account of where students come from. It is about working with parents. It is about bringing the world into schools to raise students' awareness of the world. It is about respecting diversity and inclusion of all types, ensuring a personalised learning programme in which every child has the opportunity to fulfil his or her potential irrespective of socio-economic or ethnic background.

CHAPTER TWO
What qualities make a great school leader?

In my book Teach (2015) I wrote at length about what makes a great teacher. In short, I said that great teachers are relentless in their pursuit of excellence and that their language with students is infused with this sense of urgency and drive. They need not argue about expected standards of behaviour. They achieve this in different ways – sometimes through the gravitas of maturity and experience, sometimes through warm, interpersonal interactions with every student. They have the ability to explain complex concepts in ways that make sense, they ask good questions and give really good feedback – however it is done, students feel that they are learning, they know where they stand and feel confident about the process.

Great teachers, I said, know and care about their students and make personal connections. Although pedagogical and content knowledge is important, great teachers know that what matters most is how they apply that knowledge.

Great teaching is a nuanced, complex art form. And we refer to it as "teaching practice" for a reason – we are forever practising, forever striving towards excellence and expertise. And yet we will never master it. But great teachers never tire of trying new things, of taking risks. They experiment and evaluate; they try and reflect.

For a teacher to be consistently and sustainably great, however, they need to work in a school or college where there is also great leadership. Great leaders, you see, create the conditions in which teachers can thrive; they build a culture in which risk-taking is encouraged and in which teachers are freed from any unnecessary burdens to focus on teaching. This is not to say that great leaders afford their teachers complete autonomy. Indeed, great leaders create a framework in which all their colleagues are assured of providing the highest quality of teaching, learning and assessment and do so consistently.

So what is a great leader? I've already argued that great leaders are good listeners, able to care about and respond to people's needs. I said that great leaders are consistent, fair and honest, and transparent and above reproach. They are sensitive and able to show warmth and to empathise with people's concerns and worries, and they give quality time to people. Although, when a situation requires it, they can be assertive, determined and strong, they are always kind and calm and courageous.

In addition, great leaders are not consumed by what other people think. That's not to say they are insensitive machines with skin thicker than a Tolstoy novel but that they are resilient and guided by their organisation's shared vision, as well as by their own determination and commitment to make a genuine and positive difference to people's lives. No setback will deter great leaders from achieving this vision.

However, resilience is not synonymous with an absence of empathy or social skills. Great leaders also have high EQs, that is to say they are emotionally intelligent. Some might argue that understanding how people tick is a more crucial to a leader's success than being highly intelligent, that EQ trumps IQ.

The best leaders, in my experience, do not themselves possess all of the answers, they just ask all of the right questions.

Sir Tim Brighouse – former Chief Advisor to London Schools – has wise words to share on what makes a school leader successful. In Jigsaw of a Successful School (2006), he says that successful school leaders have three qualities in common: energy, enthusiasm and hope. To this excellent list I'd add 'kindness'.

So what do these four qualities mean in practice...

Energy

Energy

To my mind, leaders need to possess resilience and determination, plus an indomitable will and passion for success. They need to show an interest in every aspect of their organisation, visiting all areas and speaking to all staff as often as possible. For example, standing in the foyer first thing in the morning allows leaders to greet staff who can then book a meeting later in the day if they need to talk. Shadowing a student once a term enables leaders to see their school from the student's point of view – an invaluable and humbling exercise.

Great leaders need to stay calm during moments of crisis, and at such times need to be willing to acknowledge mistakes that have been made and then learn from them.

Finally, great leaders need excellent time management skills and that means using the diary effectively, delegating where appropriate and protecting their precious time. By managing their time well, great leaders can use the timetabled day to walk and talk, and downtime to read and respond to emails and letters, and to do paperwork.

Enthusiasm

Enthusiasm

Great leaders need positivity, especially when communicating their organisation's vision and when reminding staff of past success as well as future promise. Such positivity can be exuded in state of the nation addresses such as assemblies, staff briefings, professional development events, and open evenings in which the leader gives a Henry V-style speech (in Shakespeare's play, Henry V rouses his army as they go into battle at Agincourt with the words, "We few, we happy few, we band of brothers; / For he today that shed his blood with me / Shall be my brother").

Great leaders need to have an intellectual curiosity, too, reading widely and sharing articles with colleagues. They also need to lead by example, as a great practitioner where appropriate, but always as someone who loves to learn and always strives to know more and be more effective. Great leaders can also be role models by performing well in assemblies, by visiting tutorials and lessons to talk to students, and by covering lessons for colleagues to allow them to engage in quality professional development.

Hope

Hope

Great leaders need to display a certainty that their vision will be realised, as if they expect it to be achieved rather than just wish it to be so. They should always seek improvement and keep colleagues focused on the process of improvement by describing the journey from the past to the present (what have colleagues already achieved?) and from the present to the future (what is their next challenge?).

Kindness

Kindness

Great leaders need to routinely recognise and reward success in a way favoured by each member of staff (some people like public adulation; others melt into a puddle at the mere thought of it). Celebrating others' achievements should be an everyday part of what these leaders do rather than an afterthought or rarity. They also need to give quality time to people, having an open door policy does not mean being available twenty-four hours a day, but it does mean being able to meet with staff as soon as possible and listening and responding to what they have to say.

Great leaders need to be protective of their staff, showing empathy, respecting people's privacy, remembering birthdays, and granting personal leave – without question – when staff have important or urgent personal matters to attend to such as family funerals. They should also set as their default position a genuine belief that everybody wishes to do well and will try their best, rather than assuming the worst of people.

*

And that, in my opinion, is what makes a great leader. But great leaders are also great because – like great teachers – they are human. And as humans they are fallible. They make mistakes. They do not always get it right.

Do not look to your leaders for perfection or expect it of yourself because, where you ostensibly find it, it may mask duplicity or inaction. Instead, look for humanity, for people who are energetic, enthusiastic, hopeful and kind but people who are also prone to making mistakes from time to time because they, like great teachers, are willing to take risks, to try new things, and to challenge and reform working practices in the hope of improving their provision. What sets these people out from the ineffectual is their willingness to admit their mistakes and their ability to learn from them, to dust themselves down, pick themselves up and keep moving forwards with energy, enthusiasm, hope and kindness.

CHAPTER THREE
How can school leaders strike a work life balance?

The qualities and skills listed above are all vital weapons in a senior leader's armoury but it is also important that leaders retain perspective and lead healthy lifestyles if they are to cope with the demands of the job and achieve longevity. The term 'work-life balance' is frequently used but, in my experience, rarely understood. Leaders accept that it is healthy to have a life outside of work but rarely acknowledge that this is also a sign of increased effectiveness. Too many people think that keeping sensible working hours is a sign of laziness or is symptomatic of a lack of commitment. Some people measure a leader's ability by how early his or her car pulls into the car park and by what time of night it drives away again. Nothing could be further from the truth.

The phrase 'work smarter not harder' may have become a hackneyed cliché but its sentiment remains as true today as it has always been. We all know colleagues who boast about the long hours they work. They tell us they've been in school since 6 o'clock that morning and didn't leave the office until 7 o'clock the previous night as if this is, in some way, a measure of ability or effectiveness. They wear their work ethic like a medal, proud to be so industrious. Like Boxer in George Orwell's 'Animal Farm' they find just one answer to every problem: 'I must work harder'. But let us take a quick walk through some of modern history's greatest achievements…

Every time there's been a significant and lasting improvement in the way we work (be that in terms of efficiency, revenue-generation or workers' conditions) it has been brought about, not by working harder, but by working smarter. The agricultural revolution, the industrial revolution and the technological revolution are perhaps the clearest examples of moments in history when the world of work has been, well, revolutionised for the better. And each revolution has been about inventing a way of working smarter: be that by developing better tools, by improving our knowledge and understanding, or by improving the quality of our communications.

For example, the increases in productivity and output brought about by the agricultural revolution were the result of advances in science, engineering and botany such as: enclosure, mechanisation, crop-rotation systems, and selective breeding. These were ways of working smarter; they did not result in farmers having to work longer hours – indeed, Jethro Tull's seed drill reduced the amount of labour required to plough and sow fields.

Equally, the industrial revolution – during which time income grew tenfold and the population grew sixfold – was about changes in technology and transport. It's true to say that the effects of the industrial revolution on working conditions were not immediate – it was not untypical for millworkers to work 10 hours a day during the 19th century – but the invention of machines fuelled by water and steam gradually led to improved conditions. The concentration of labour in mechanised mills also improved the organisation of labour which allowed trade unions to fight for improved working conditions. Later, trains, ships, and the internal combustion engine improved trade which gave further momentum to economic progress.

The technological revolution – a phrase often used to describe a second wave of industrial revolution corresponding to the latter half of the 19th century but here used to describe the advancement of information and communications technology in the latter half of the 20th century and early part of the 21st century – has continued in this vein. The personal computer, the mobile phone, email, internet and social networking have all helped us to work smarter and, crucially, to work fewer hours. Communication is now instantaneous; we are able to share information more readily.

As a result of the agricultural revolution, the industrial revolution and the technological revolution we are able to work smarter not harder. And we need to learn the lessons of the last few hundred years and realise that effective organisation and appropriate delegation are signs of a successful, skilled leader; working twelve hours a day are not.

Working unsocial hours – depriving oneself of a life outside of work – is a measure of one's ineffectiveness. An effective school leader should be able to manage his or her time effectively and delegate appropriately in order to fulfil his or her duties within reasonable working hours. Organisation and delegation are basic management skills, after all. Moreover, an effective school leader should model a healthy work-life balance. An effective school leader should lead by example in showing his or her colleagues that it is important to have a life outside of work because doing so increases a person's sense of perspective and improves their quality of judgment. It helps to minimise stress.

Enjoying a life outside of work adds to a person's life experiences and frame of reference. They can relate to colleagues and to students more readily if they experience life outside of school. At its simplest level, watching last night's episode of Coronation Street gives you a shared experience with colleagues and students – you have something with which to connect to other people. Spending time with family or friends, allowing the events of the day to melt away, allows you to distance yourself from those events and therefore to establish some perspective about their relative importance.

That is not to say the events that seem of vital importance by day become irrelevant by night. As a school leader you deal with serious matters which require serious thought and care. But it is right that school leaders remain detached – emotionally speaking – and are able to make logical, strategic decisions which stand up to long-term scrutiny; not rash decisions of the heart, decisions taken under stress.

Let me make clear that being a school leader is not just a job: it is a career and something you should feel passionately about. It is important that school leaders do their jobs well. But that does not mean they should work all hours of day and night; nor does it mean they would be better at their jobs and get more done if they did so.

So, how do school leaders strike the right work-life balance? Everyone has a different way of working but being organised is clearly at the heart of it. There are various ways to organise your workload and I discuss many of them in this book. Here are just three examples with which to begin:

Keep lists
Prioritise tasks according to their importance and timescale; make informed decisions about the relative impact of the actions that are asked of you upon students' learning and well-being. For example, use a 1 to 3 scale (or traffic lights) whereby 1 is urgent (usually to be completed within 24 hours), 2 is important (within 2 to 3 days) and 3 is neutral (ideally by the end of the week but often by the end of the month or half-term). There should be a fourth category: items to be delegated.

Delegate
Knowing which tasks can be delegated and to whom is important; keeping track of those tasks – striking the right balance between giving colleagues

genuine ownership of the task and ensuring it is completed on time – is also important.

Keep meetings short and productive

This can be done by circulating a clear, agreed agenda prior to the meeting and doggedly sticking to that agenda, ensuring that deviations are avoided. The minutes of meetings should be short and should list the actions required and the people responsible for their completion. Meetings are often important, unavoidable and the most effective way of making decisions. But knowing when a meeting is necessary and when meetings can be avoided is just as important. Ask yourself: can I achieve the same outcome without a meeting? Can the matter be resolved by email, a telephone call or a 'walk and talk'? If a meeting is necessary, what is the best format? A formal, round the table meeting or a short, standing briefing? Colleagues will respond better to meetings if they know they are only held when necessary.

*

Postscript to Chapter Three

When I wrote the first edition of this book back in 2010, I argued - in the chapter on work life balance which you've just read - that making time for yourself and switching off from work was not only good for your health but was also crucial to increasing your effectiveness as a leader. I said that working unsocial hours and depriving yourself of a life outside of school was a measure of ineffectiveness because a good school leader should be able to manage his or her time effectively. Enjoying a life outside of work, I added, expands one's life experiences and increases one's frame of reference.

Since I wrote that chapter, new research has emerged which suggests that striking a work life balance is not only heathy, it also improves your thinking skills and creativity.

In The Seven Habits of Highly Effective People, Stephen Covey talks about 'sharpening the saw'. If you spend the whole day sawing wood but don't find time to sharpen your saw, Covey says, then your work will suffer. In other words, as leaders we need to take care of our most vital leadership resources: our physical, social, and mental wellbeing, because it is these resources that enable us to be energetic, enthusiastic, hopeful and kind.

The German car manufacturer Volkswagen has taken dramatic steps to promote a healthy work life balance and ensure its workers 'sharpen the saw'. They now block emails after office hours - they shut the servers so no one can send or receive emails in the evenings and at weekends - and only open them up again, thus releasing to workers' inboxes any external emails that were sent during 'lockdown', at the start of the next working day.

What downtime allows us to do is incubate ideas. When we switch off from work, our mind steps back from doing and is allowed to reflect and think - often subconsciously and in the background.

Mihaly Csikszentmihalyi has studied the most creatively prolific people in a variety of fields and he found that everyone he interviewed described the same five-stage process, namely:

1. Research
2. Incubation
3. Insight and ideation
4. Evaluation
5. Elaboration

The most productive and creative people, Csikszentmihalyi concluded, began by conducting research, working out what questions to ask, developing an understanding of the background to those questions. Then they made time for 'incubation' - they stepped away from the problem that occupied the space at the front of their minds and allowed it to push back into their subconscious whilst they worked on something else.

Many leaders who juggle various projects or problems at any one time - and that invariably means all school leaders - find that incubation takes place naturally because if they switch to a different project or switch off from work, they incubate the project or problem they were just working on.

The third stage is a period of insight - the lightbulb moment. Sometimes when leaders have placed ideas into incubation by switching off, something clicks in their subconscious and everything comes together naturally and this pulls them out of incubation and into insight. Other times, leaders have to force ideas out of incubation and into insight. They do this through ideation - such as brainstorming. Even if ideation has to be forced, the research suggests that leaders have more and better ideas when they've had a period of incubation.

Incubation doesn't have to take place over weeks or even days. In fact, ideas can incubate in as little as five minutes or during a short walk.

According to Csikszentmihalyi's research, the next stages after insight are evaluation followed by elaboration. First, leaders assess the validity and quality of their insights - are the solutions they've come up with any good? Will they work in practice? Are they achievable? Elaboration, the final stage, is the process of putting a solution into practice, trying it out for real.

The most crucial stage is incubation for this is where ideas are created and shaped. But if you don't find time to switch off and think actively, if you never step away from your work emails, for example, because you have a smart phone that follows you everywhere and allows emails to intrude into your every waking moment, then you'll never be able to incubate properly. This is why you shouldn't take your work home with you - or at least not every evening and weekend. It's why you should draw some boundaries and make some time for you and for other interests. Exercise is a great way to kickstart the incubation period, as is socialising with family and friends.

Making a change to your daily routines is always difficult and if you set yourself a goal that's unrealistic, it simply won't happy.

This is why you shouldn't - if you're a workaholic who never switches off - attempt to make a sweeping change such as vowing never to take work home with you or committing to blocking all work emails between the hours of 6pm and 8am the following day.

What you need to do, if you are to make a change that you stick to and that works, is develop 'micro-goals'…

Micro-goals, sometimes called mini-habits, are routines with a small, simple goal. For example, rather than committing to read a novel every week, you commit to read two pages of a book every evening before bedtime. Rather than promising yourself you'll cut out caffeinated drinks, you promise to replace one cup of coffee a day with a glass of water.

Although micro-goals might seem pointless, the very fact that they are realistic and achievable is what makes them powerful. You need very little willpower to meet a micro-goal and so your chances of succeeding are vastly improved, and the chances of failure are negligible.

Psychologically, micro-goals afford you the daily feeling of success, and this affirmation is crucial if you are to embed a new routine.

So how do micro-goals work in practice?

First, you must choose the right habits to form. Your micro-goal must be related to something you really want to achieve and that you know will improve your lifestyle or effectiveness. For example, if you want to learn a foreign language, you should set a micro-goal of learning one new word a day.

Second, you must create 'cues'. A cue is a feeling or an action that reminds you to meet your micro-goal. For example, every time you clean your teeth, you learn a new word. That ensures you set a fixed time of the day to work towards your micro-goal and your brain connects the act of cleaning your teeth with the act of learning a new word. The two soon become inextricably linked and the chances of you forgetting to learn a word or deciding that today is not the day to do so, are greatly reduced if not eradicated altogether.

Third, you need to track how well you're doing against your micro-goal. You do this by reflecting on your daily achievements - did you succeed? What did you achieve? How does it feel? How has it enriched your life? Conducting a short self-evaluation of this nature will help you stick to your new routine and give you a sense of reward and recognition. It will also encourage you to commit to a second then a third micro-goal.

So follow the evidence and ensure you find time every day to switch off from work, to distance yourself from emails, and allow ideas to incubate, thus improving your productivity and creativity. Commit to small goals every day that enable you to develop these new routines - such as switching your mobile phone off for half an hour every evening, then for an hour, then turning off all email notifications between the hours of 7pm and 7am. With small steps you will walk a marathon; with each little victory you will win a battle and then the war.

Try it today.

CHAPTER FOUR
Why do great school leaders need a vision?

How can senior leaders – whilst displaying the qualities and skills discussed earlier – help bring about school improvement?

Firstly, it is the responsibility of school leaders to create effective structures in which:
- there is a clear vision of what you're trying to achieve
- targets are realistic and achievable
- true delegation is offered and senior staff are empowered to make decisions
- effective systems of communication are in place;
- purposeful meetings are called; meetings are minuted and actions set
- paper work is kept to a minimum
- all staff know exactly who does what
- actions are delivered within the context of the school improvement plan
- students are at the centre of any decisions and changes
- there are effective monitoring and evaluative procedures in place at all levels
- there is clear value for money in terms of the school's effectiveness and efficiency.

Let's start at the beginning of this list with vision...

What's the difference between a vision statement and a mission statement?

I find it useful to think of the two terms, which are often used interchangeably, in the following way: vision is your destination; mission is your means of transport.

In other words, a vision statement sets out what you want your school to be like whereas a mission statement articulates the behaviours and values, systems and processes, you expect your school to adopt in order to get there.

Vision is your *destination*

Mission is your *means of transport*

What makes a good vision statement?

One of the five dimensions of what Vivianne Robinson calls 'student-centred leadership' is establishing goals and expectations. "In a world where everything seems important, or at least important to someone," she says, "goal setting enables leaders to sort through the multiple demands to establish the relative importance of these various demands and thus provide a clear steer for an otherwise rudderless ship".

Goal setting in education, Robinson argues, is not about deciding what is and is not important. Goal setting works because it forces decisions about relative importance – about what is more important in this context, at this time, than all the other important things.

Establishing and articulating clear goals – what we might call our 'vision' – is crucial for any organisation but particularly important for schools which – you might say – sail on such troubled waters, tugged – as they are – back and forth on a tide of policy from successive governments and their quangos.

A vision makes explicit what an organisation stands for and what its people want it to achieve; it binds people (staff, students, governors, the community, employers, and so on) together in the pursuit of a common goal and reminds them why they do what they do every day. A vision provides a focus for decision-making and conveys a picture of what the future will look like.

According to John Kotter in his book, Leading Change, an effective vision is desirable in that it appeals to the long-term interests of employees, customers, stockholders, and others who have a stake in the enterprise. It is feasible in that it comprises realistic, attainable goals and is focused in that it is clear enough to provide guidance in decision making. An effective vision is also flexible in that it is general enough to allow individual initiative and alternative responses in light of changing conditions. It is also communicable. In other words, it is easy to communicate and can be successfully explained within five minutes.

The most effective vision statements, Kotter says, also share the following characteristics…

They are ambitious enough to force people out of comfortable routines. For example, becoming 5 per cent better is not the goal; becoming the best at something is often the goal.

They aim in a general way at providing better and better products or services at lower and lower costs, thus appealing greatly to customers and stockholders.

They take advantage of fundamental trends, especially globalisation and new technology.

And they make no attempt to exploit anyone and thus have a certain moral power.

For my part, I believe an effective vision is one which is shared – not just in the sense that it is communicated but that it is understood and owned by most (if not all) of the people in the organisation. It is all well and good for a leader to have a clear vision of what he or she wants to achieve but it will forever remain an aspiration and will never be achieved if it is not understood and shared by everyone else in the organisation.

In schools, a vision will only be realised if every teacher, every teaching assistant, every member of support staff, and every middle and senior leader makes it happen through their everyday behaviours and actions. It is no use having a vision which many staff disagree with or misunderstand, or which does not suit the organisation's context. It has to make sense, be achievable and be meaningful. It has to take the organisation forward in the right direction. It has to be something that everyone wants to see take shape. In other words, it has to benefit everyone.

Ideally, a vision statement should express what is unique about an organisation and not be an 'off-the-peg' statement which could easily be applied to any school in any part of the country or indeed the world. What are the unique challenges the organisation needs to overcome? What will success look like for that particular institution? What makes its stakeholders different?

A good starting point when writing a vision statement, therefore, is the organisation's existing vision or, if it does not have one, its motto or values. Why? Because although a vision statement is about the future, it should have solid foundations in the past, in the organisation's history, in what the organisation stands for and in the very reason it exists. Continuity is important to all those with a stake in the place. No one likes change; it is uncomfortable. People like to know that what they have built, what they have worked hard for, what they believe in, is to be retained and protected. A vision which refers to what the organisation already does well as well as articulates what it hopes to do better in the future keeps all parties happy. Moreover, it is balanced, fair and, above all, cohesive: it connects stakeholders along a path which leads from the past, through the present, to the future.

On the subject of cohesion, all stakeholders (staff, students, governors, the community, etc.) need to be involved in agreeing the vision but this does not have to mean a long and convoluted process of wrangling over every word. Instead, the senior team – or perhaps a working party representing as many different areas of the organisation as possible – should draft a vision for wider consultation. That consultation should be clearly framed: what aspects of the vision are leaders consulting on, what are the dividing lines? Leaders need to make it clear what is open for debate and what is not. Do they want to debate every word or do they want to debate broad principles?

Leaders need to make clear what form they expect the consultation to take and how they will garner feedback. They need to make clear how they will respond to that feedback. People need to feel listened to but, equally, leaders should not promise something they cannot deliver.

As well as the organisation's existing vision, motto or values, the vision should be informed by the current (3-year) priorities or targets which in turn (in the case of schools), are likely to be informed by their latest inspection report, their latest exam results and an analysis of 3-year trends, and a review of the latest school improvement plan.

Kotter says that the process of creating an effective vision often starts with an initial statement from a single individual, reflecting both his or her dreams and real marketplace needs. The first draft is always modelled over time by a guiding coalition of senior leaders or an even larger group of influential people. Teamwork is important. The group process never works well without a minimum of effective teamwork. The head and the heart have roles of equal importance: analytical thinking and a lot of dreaming are – Kotter says – essential throughout the process of creating a vision.

The process can often be messy because vision-creation is usually a process of two steps forward and one back, movement to the left and then to the right. Vision is never created in a single meeting. The activity takes months, sometimes years. The process results in a direction for the future that is desirable, feasible, focused, flexible, and is conveyable in five minutes or less.

Robinson says that, in terms of creating a vision, three conditions need to be in place. People need to feel personally committed to the goal and believe they have the capacity to achieve it. The goal also needs to be specific so people can monitor their progress towards it. Vision creation (or 'goal setting' as Robinson calls it) works by creating a discrepancy between the current situation and an attractive future. This discrepancy motivates people to focus their effort and attention on the activities required to reach the goal and to persist until they achieve it.

People commit to a vision that they believe is important. Robinson says that the pursuit of the goal becomes attractive because it provides an opportunity for reducing the gap between the vision and the current reality. This means that two things are required for goal commitment. The goal needs to provide an opportunity to achieve what is valued, and people need to accept that the current situation falls sufficiently short of that vision to warrant pursuit of the goal. This is why it is important that a vision is a collective goal rather than that of a single leader and that it emerges through discussion rather than being imposed.

The second aspect of gaining goal commitment, according to Robinson, is acceptance of the gap between the goal and the existing state of affairs. "Many leaders...focus only on the desirability of the goal and not on the difference between what they envisage and the present situation," she argues. One solution, Robinson says, is to engage in 'constructive problem talk': "Such talk involves naming, describing, and analysing problems in ways that reveal the possibilities for change. Constructive problem talk builds trust because people respect leadership that can own problems and take responsibility for solving them."

Creating a vision works best when people are committed to goals which they believe they have the capacity to achieve. Commitment and capacity are highly interdependent because people will not commit to goals which they believe they cannot achieve.

"When the responsible system lacks the capacity to achieve a particular goal," Robinson says, "leaders should initially set learning rather than performance goals". Performance goals are about "the achievement of a specific outcome". A learning goal, by contrast, focuses on the "discovery of the strategies, processes, or procedures to perform the task effectively". With a learning goal, attention is directed to learning how to do the task rather than to achieving a specific outcome.

According to Robinson, a vision is specific when it "include[s] criteria by which progress and achievement can be judged". Ensuring the vision has a set of SMART targets or objectives attached to it makes sense because people cannot regulate their performance if they are unclear about how to assess their progress.

However, Robinson argues that there are occasions when the call to set SMART targets is inappropriate: "In order to set a SMART goal, you have to know quite a lot about how to achieve it. When goals involve new challenges, how can you possibly know if it is achievable, if it is realistic, and how long it will take you to achieve it?"

A vision should also be clearly focused because if it has too many goals it will defeat the purpose of giving clear messages about what takes priority.

An additional challenge in achieving goals is developing the routines that enable teachers to integrate goal pursuit into their daily work. Without such routines, a 'business as usual' mentality and approach will drive goal achievement.

Let us now to consider the mission statement…

As I say above, the vision is the destination and the mission is the means of transport. The mission is necessarily longer than the vision statement because it is a detailed declaration of what an organisation will do in order to achieve its vision. A mission statement should try to cover all the important aspects of an organisation's working practices. In the case of schools, for example, it might cover: how it uses data; what kind of curriculum it has or aspires to have; what the atmosphere should be like; how it caters for vulnerable students; how it engages with the local community; and so on.

As a starting point, consider the following statements:

Our school is a place where…

- there is a shared vision of what the school is trying to achieve;
- data is understood and acted upon appropriately;
- students make good or better progress within each year and key stage, academically, emotionally and socially;
- there is a rich curriculum taught by skilled, well-motivated teachers;
- there is a purposeful, organised working atmosphere, students are valued and their contributions are appreciated;
- resources, including quality ICT provision, are well-matched to the curriculum;
- students are challenged and encouraged to do their best;
- vulnerable children are identified early and support mechanisms are put in place;
- parents are fully informed and are welcomed contributors to school life;
- there is a sense of involvement in the local community and visitors and outside agencies provide contributions to the school;
- all staff are valued and are supported in their own personal and professional development;
- standards reflect the status of the students: there is no coasting, and realistic achievement targets are consistently met;
- the school is held in high esteem by the local community;
- there is appropriate and interesting extra-curricular provision.

Once the vision and mission have been agreed, they need to be officially ratified by governors. Once ratified, they should not be filed away in a dusty drawer and forgotten about. They should be placed centre-stage. They should be referred to as frequently as possible, in as many different ways as possible, and should underpin everything the organisation does.

In practice, this might mean:

- Including the vision statement on letter-headed paper, in a prospectus, and in newsletters and leaflets
- Using the vision to frame the organisation's 3-year strategy, aims and objectives
- Including the vision and mission on the front page of the school improvement plan (SIP) and using it to frame that plan: a section for each aspect of the vision, broken down into specific actions which will help to realise the vision
- Including the vision and mission on the front page of the self-evaluation form (SEF)
- Including the vision and mission in faculty or departmental action plans
- Including the vision in performance management documentation and using the vision to provide a broad basis for staff appraisal objectives

In Student-Centred Leadership, Robinson, for her part, says that, "once clear goals are established, the second dimension of effective leadership – resourcing strategically – comes into play". In other words, the vision or goal should be used to determine what to spend an organisation's precious time and money on.

"Scarce resources – money, time, teaching materials, and instructional expertise – [should be] allocated in ways that give priority to key goals," she says. "As such, strategic resourcing and strategic thinking are closely linked: strategic thinking involves asking questions and challenging assumptions about the links between resources and the needs they are intended to meet."

Kotter says that a vision can get lost in the clutter of everyday working life if leaders fail to communicate it effectively. The total amount of communication going to an employee in three months, he argues, is approximately 2,300,000 words or numbers. The typical communication of a change vision over a period of three months equates to just 13,400 words or numbers (that is, the equivalent of one 30-minute speech, one hour-long meeting, one 600-word article in the firm's newspaper, and one 2,000-word memo). This means that the change vision captures only 0.58 per cent of the communication market share.

In order to communicate the vision more effectively, then, leaders need to ensure communications are simple – all jargon and technobabble must be eliminated. Leaders need to make use of metaphor, analogy, and example: a verbal picture, after all, paints a thousand words. Leaders need to use multiple forums such as meetings (big and small), memos and newsletters, formal and informal interaction – all are effective means of spreading the word. Repetition is also key: ideas sink in deeply only after they have been heard many times - seven times in seven different ways is a good rule of thumb.

Leaders need to lead by example because if the behaviour of important people is inconsistent with the vision, it will overwhelm all other forms of communication. Leaders need to explain seeming inconsistencies because, if inconsistencies go unaddressed, they will undermine the credibility of all other communications. And finally, leaders need to allow for a bit of 'give-and-take', a bit of two-way communication because a dialogue is always more effective than a monologue. It's the 'con' in 'conversation', after all: 'con' meaning 'with' in Italian.

So use the vision to frame every conversation and speech, to focus every meeting, to inform every decision. Use it as a mantra. It will remind people of their ultimate goal and refocus them on what's most important; it will convince them that they are playing a crucial role in helping to make the organisation's vision a reality and reassure them that they are helping to shape the future.

*

Daniel Coyle, in his book The Culture Code, argues that there are four types of 'catchphrase' which he calls the North Star, Do's, Don'ts, and Identity.

The North Star provides the Why. It has the highest priority because it carries the aim or objective. In other words, the North Star is the vision.

The Do's and Don'ts, meanwhile, describe the How. In other words, they articulate how to achieve the aim or objective.

The Identity outlines the qualities or traits that distinguish the organisation from the rest of the world. In other words, they articulate the Who - the personality, morals, beliefs and attitudes of the organisation, and what makes them unique.

Taken together, these four types of 'catchphrase' create what Coyle calls the "culture story". This captures the soul of the group — or, as Coyle puts it, "a narrative algorithm that provides the crucial connections between the Why, the Who, the How".

In other words, catchphrases - and vision statements - aren't cliched or corny; they are genius because purpose isn't just about inspiration, it's also about navigation. Having a shared purpose is about building a vivid, accessible roadmap with a set of emotional GPS signals that define the organisation's identity and guide the behaviour of its staff.

CHAPTER FIVE
Why does school improvement require leaders not managers?

Once you have a vision and mission, you need to begin the process of school improvement. The steps you take on the journey depend, in large part, on your starting point and initial destination. Getting from 'inadequate' to 'requires improvement' is different than moving from 'requires improvement' to 'good' which is, in turn, different than the journey to 'outstanding'. As such, we will consider each of these three 'journeys' in the next few chapters.

In Chapter Six we will look at transforming failing schools. Then, in Chapter Seven, we will look at 'getting to good'. Finally, in Chapter Eight, we will consider the 'journey to outstanding'. But first let us consider some of the general principles involved in school improvement...

Leaders not managers

Schools need leaders not managers to oversee the process of school improvement.

Leadership and management are words often glued together like 'salt and pepper' and 'knife and fork' but they are actually quite different. Yes, it is true that most leaders are appointed because they have a proven track record as good managers; and, yes, it is true that good leaders need to continue practising their management skills. But nevertheless the two are different. Whereas managers bring order and organisation; leaders bring change and challenges. Managers are concerned with the short-term; leaders with the long-term. Managers solve problems and achieve goals; leaders pose questions and generate options and opportunities.

Put simply:
- managers are operational, and
- leaders are strategic.

I introduced two types of senior leadership team (SLT) meeting at one of my previous schools: SLT 'strategy' meetings which took place after school as part of the whole-school meeting cycle (about once every three weeks) and SLT 'operational' meetings which took place within the school day (and once a week).

The agenda for these meetings were distinct: strategy meetings were concerned with long-term planning and were focused on discussions around the school improvement plan – where we are and where we're going, and often resulted in updates to the SEF; operational meetings were concerned with the here and now, with what had happened over the previous week and what was coming up in the next week.

Strategy meetings were about vision and mission, creating a long-term plan and articulating what we aspired to achieve in the future; operational meetings were about the day-to-day running of a school, solving yesterday's problems for tomorrow. In other words, strategy meetings were about leadership; operational meetings were about management. I found the distinction helpful.

Managers need a range of skills including: communication, organisation, operational leadership, managing difficult staff and managing difficult situations.

Leaders need strategic vision (to be able to see clearly where they and their school are going, to be able to aim high and share their passion and determination with others, to be able to communicate their plans with enthusiasm and clarity) and strategic planning (knowing where their school is now, where they want to go and how they're going to get there).

As I say above, schools need effective senior leaders to drive school improvement. They must distribute leadership and empower others to make decisions, they must not micro-manage every goal and target on the school improvement plan. They need oversight, they need to be able to see the 'bigger picture' and draw various elements together. They do not need to know all the details, just be reassured that someone else does.

Two starting principles of school improvement

1. Talk isn't cheap...

Leaders of school improvement must talk to their staff – communication is the key to success. Staff must feel informed and involved in the process of improvement. Leaders should be open and honest with colleagues and should seek to reach agreement where possible but should not be afraid to make difficult – perhaps unpopular – decisions when this is right for the school.

Leaders must not abdicate responsibility but should share it. Where a decision is taken which is not consensual, the rationale should be clearly explained and staff should understand the benefits of that decision for the school and its students.

Leaders should not see it as a weakness to ask for help or advice from colleagues or others; nor should they be afraid to admit when they get it wrong. It is a strength, not a weakness, to be self-aware and pragmatic, to adapt to changing circumstances and respond to evolving situations.

2. Tweak not transform…

Change is uncomfortable and unsettling. People are not at their best when experiencing change. Not only should leaders be open and honest about the changes that are needed; not only should they communicate the rationale behind change and outline the benefits of change; they should also try to avoid unnecessary change.

It is important to understand the status quo, to know what works well and what should be protected and retained. It is important to identify the foundations on which to build. People do not like change because it is uncomfortable and challenging. People like to know their hard work has purpose and meaning. Change needs to be incremental; the future needs to be built on the foundations of the past.

Here's a short aside on the subject of 'tweaking'…

One of the great puzzles of the industrial revolution is why it began in England and not, say, France or Germany. The economists Ralf Meisenzahl and Joel Mokyr believe that Britain's advantage was in its human-capital. In particular, they argue that Britain had a great group of "tweakers" that gave it the edge.

These tweakers were resourceful and creative men who took the signature inventions of the industrial age and tweaked them. In other words, they took existing ideas and refined and perfected them, and made them work.

In 1779, Samuel Crompton of Lancashire invented the spinning mule, which made the mechanisation of cotton manufacture possible. And yet England's real advantage over other industrialising nations was that it also had Henry Stones of Horwich who added metal rollers to Crompton's mule. England also had James Hargreaves of Tottington who worked out how to smooth the acceleration and deceleration of the spinning wheel. Then William Kelly of Glasgow worked out how to add water power to the draw stroke, and John Kennedy of Manchester who adapted the wheel to turn out fine counts. And, finally, Richard Roberts, also of Manchester and a master of precision machine tooling, created the "automatic" spinning mule: an exacting, high-speed, reliable rethinking of Crompton's original creation.

All these men, the economists argue, provided the "micro inventions [that were] necessary to make macro inventions highly productive and remunerative."

The crux of Meisenzahl and Mokyr's argument is that this sort of tweaking was what made Britain the world leader in the Nineteenth Century. And it remains this sort of tweaking that is essential if we are to make progress today.

James Watt invented the modern steam engine, doubling the efficiency of the engines that had come before. But when the so-called 'tweakers' got involved, the efficiency of the steam engine quadrupled.

Samuel Crompton was responsible for what Meisenzahl and Mokyr call "arguably the most productive invention" of the industrial revolution but the key moment in the history of the mule came a few years later when there was a strike of cotton workers.

The mill owners were looking for a way to replace the workers with unskilled labour, and needed an automatic mule which did not need to be controlled by the spinner. And who solved the problem? Not Crompton but the tweaker's tweaker Richard Roberts who, in 1825, produced a prototype and, in 1830, manufactured an even better solution.

As a result, the number of spindles on a typical mule jumped from four hundred to a thousand.

The tweakers are what put Britain at the epicentre of the industrial revolution. And the best school leaders have learned the lesson of history. They know that the best way to achieve genuine, sustainable improvements is to tweak and not transform. They know that change should be incremental and that the future should be built on the foundations of the past.

CHAPTER SIX
How can leaders transform a failing school?

Although - as I argued in the last chapter - genuine, sustainable school improvement is a slow, incremental process achieved by tweaking not transforming, time is often in short supply for those schools judged inadequate or placed into 'special measures'. It is easy for those schools judged 'good' or 'outstanding' - with the freedom and time that such judgments bring - to tweak at the edges of their performance. But when a school is deemed to be failing, freedom and time are luxuries they can ill afford.

The unrelenting cycle of Ofsted inspections can put huge pressure on headteachers/principals and their senior teams to demonstrate rapidly rising standards before a government academy broker comes knocking at the door intent on sweeping away the school's governance and leadership with their new broom.

What, then, is the secret to turning around an underperforming school in a relatively short space of time, whilst also laying down firm foundations for sustainable improvements? Here are four suggestions...

1. Change school leadership practices

Firstly, assuming the existing leadership team remains in post, senior staff need to overtly change their leadership practices. Senior leaders need to become 'instructional leaders', highly visible around the school and in classrooms; leading by example as excellent teachers first, administrators second. After all, standards can only improve if changes are made in the classroom - learning does not take place in offices and boardrooms; it takes place in lessons, in the space between the teacher and students.

As such, senior leaders should put pedagogy first - accepting that high quality teaching and learning in the classroom trumps all - and signal this in tangible ways by removing as many of the distractions that teachers face as they feasibly can, maximising the amount of time they spend in the classroom with students.

If teaching and learning is of the highest quality, there will be less need of bolt-on intervention strategies outside of the classroom and outside of school hours, and more chance of students' socio-economic differences being rendered null and void. As Hamre and Pianta's research (2005) found, in classrooms run by the most effective teachers, disadvantaged students progress at the same rate as non-disadvantaged students.

The senior team also need to continually communicate their improvement plans to all of the school's stakeholders and then ensure they make each tangible improvement public. They can do this by consulting on, agreeing and communicating a new vision and mission for the school, and by using this to remind staff, students and parents of the school's purpose. This vision must be premised on the notion of high expectations for all, and build on strong values of educational excellence and fair access, affording every student an equal opportunity to achieve his or her potential.

Strong leadership teams also share leadership. This is not the same as delegating tasks or actions; it means genuinely empowering all staff - and indeed the student body - with 'real' leadership and authority.

Senior leaders can also change their leadership practices by building a consensus amongst their staff, forging a cohesive culture in which everybody works towards the same end goal. Senior leaders should recognise the need to change and possess a willingness to try new things to raise student performance. This willingness can come from a study of school improvement theory, research, and practice. Of course, changing leadership practices isn't always easy. Some staff may need to be convinced that the school has the potential to change and will change.

Some staff - like Benjamin the donkey in George Orwell's Animal Farm - believe that reforms will 'come and go' so patiently 'wait out' the latest set of changes. To combat this, senior leaders in the school should couple signaling change with publicly celebrating quick wins. Signalling change may also be difficult if the prevailing perception of the school by the local community is negative. School leaders may need to initiate a public PR campaign. For example, the headteacher/principal could hold early morning meetings with parents when they drop their children off at school and could invite parents to spend time in the school, watching lessons and observing special events and activities.

2. Use data to improve teaching and learning

Secondly, schools in search of rapid improvement should examine their achievement data in order to identify specific gaps in students' learning and progress. They should ensure that every teacher uses formative data about individual students in order to analyse the effectiveness of their teaching.

Data should be used to identify the one or two priority areas for improving the quality of teaching, learning and assessment. Senior leaders should then invest in targeted professional development, differentiated according to individual teachers' needs and subject areas. The best professional development focuses on a small number of 'tweaks' and does so over the long-term. The best professional development is also collaborative and practitioner-led, grounded in research.

Staff should be encouraged and supported to work collaboratively to carry out a comprehensive review of the curriculum in order to ensure that it aligns with national and local needs and expectations, but more importantly that it meets the needs of all the students in the school.

All staff - not just senior leaders - should be responsible for monitoring and evaluating student progress and should do so regularly and systematically, making adjustments where necessary in order to strengthen teaching, as well as student learning and progress.

Underperforming schools in need of rapid improvement also need to examine student achievement data in order to identify the gaps and weaknesses in student learning. The headteacher/principal may decide to establish a data leader on the senior leadership team to organise and lead this effort. This senior leader can examine student learning through test outcomes and classroom assessments.

This senior leader can also look at the data in order to ascertain the factors that contribute to or impede student learning, such as problems with attendance and punctuality, poor discipline, problems within a student's family unit, language limitations, and so on.

As above, it's vital that senior leaders adopt the role of 'instructional leader' and are highly visible in classrooms. Strong instructional leadership demonstrates the importance of bolstering teaching and learning, the curriculum, and assessment, and shows that the senior leadership team are leading by example, leading the effort, and maintaining vigilance toward targeted, measurable goals.

School leaders should also be 'lead learners' - demonstrating the importance of engaging in professional development based on an analysis of achievement and quality data, and that's tailored to meet the needs of individual teachers and subject areas.

The best professional development also balances the necessity to improve content knowledge with the need to improve pedagogic knowledge (developing teachers' knowledge of their subject and their knowledge of how to teach that subject to young people, pre-empting students' questions and misconceptions, and explaining complex concepts in a way that makes sense to students).

Naturally, there are likely to be some 'bumps in the road' along the way to using data to improve teacher instruction. For example, data analysis may be new and unfamiliar to some teachers and they may need support in developing the requisite skills. Teachers may also fear reprisals or negative consequences if their classroom data is scrutinised.

The systematic use of data requires teachers to shift their attitudes toward solving problems. The senior team can facilitate and model this change in attitude and practice. For example, the headteacher/principal can become immersed in the data to support and guide teachers. An external advisor or consultant should also be used to facilitate this process and provide specialised training to help teachers fully understand the different types of data and ways of using this data to further student learning.

To change instructional practices and improve learning, the learning goals must be realistic, and improved practices must be sufficient and appropriate in order to produce the desired results. Any plans for improvement must be grounded in good data, understood by the whole school community, executed competently, and modified with experience.

3. Achieve 'quick wins' to motivate staff

Thirdly, senior leaders need to keep staff morale high and make ongoing improvements visible and public by sharing 'quick wins' early in the turnaround process. The best way to achieve this is to start with a goal that is important but can also be achieved quickly and can provide visible, tangible evidence of improvement. For example, changing the school's use of time (scheduling a common, weekly slot for professional development or joint lesson planning time), improving access to resources (a CPD library, subscriptions to online materials, ICT equipment, textbooks, etc.) and the physical environment (painting corridors, fixing broken fixtures and fittings, tidying up the school grounds, etc.) and improving discipline (establishing a safe and orderly environment with clear rules that are known and applied consistently by all teachers and fully supported by senior leaders) are all strategies which can yield 'quick wins'.

Another way to ensure a school achieves 'quick wins' is to identify one or two goals that build on the school's existing needs and strengths, are important to staff, and can be achieved quickly. A narrow goal such as "increasing Year 7 students' reading achievement on a high-stakes test" can be achieved faster than a broad goal such as "increasing attainment for all students in all subjects".

School leaders should also consider strategies that minimise the dependence on others for decisions or financial support. A strategy that requires external support - such as from the local authority, academy trust or government agencies - is unlikely to be implemented quickly. Similarly, changing the way teachers approach their work might require a consensus among all teaching staff and this takes time. School leaders should think about strategies that they have the authority and funds to implement and that do not require the wholesale involvement of all school staff.

As ever, there are some potential roadblocks to look out for and overcome. For example, many of the stakeholders (parents, governors, local authority and trust representatives) in an underperforming school expect all the improvement goals to be met simultaneously and immediately, making it difficult to focus on any one goal which could yield a 'quick win'. Therefore, the headteacher/principal and senior team must be willing to stay focused and determined, even when pressured to broaden the goals being pursued.

Setting a goal that is a priority for most stakeholders will ease the pressure somewhat by ensuring there is an initial base of support. Setting a short timeline for accomplishing that goal may also help. A quick win on one goal and turning immediately to other important goals can help stakeholders feel that all their concerns will eventually be addressed.

It's important to ensure that each quick win is sustained over the long-term because a quick win that is just as quickly lost becomes yet another example of the superficial and temporary nature of school reform. As such, senior leaders need to follow up the quick win with strategies to sustain its success.

For example, if money has been invested in a new CPD library for staff, it should be followed up with regular investment to keep the library up-to-date and relevant. If the corridors have been repainted and the grounds cleaned, then this should be followed up by regular inspections and an investment in ongoing maintenance.

4. Achieve a staff consensus and develop leadership capacity

Fourthly, the SLT need to ensure that all staff 'sign up' to the improvement agenda and are committed to change. An assessment could be carried out in order to identify staff who are not fully committed to the school improvement goals or who do not have the qualifications to carry them out. The SLT could redeploy staff who have valuable skills but are not effective in their current role.

It may be necessary to replace some staff members who actively resist the school's turnaround efforts and then recruit new staff who have the requisite skills and competencies. However, a headteacher/principal's starting point should be that all staff have the potential and capability to help turn the school around and any negativity or seeming lack of skill is likely the result of poor leadership and support in the past. Staff must be afforded fair opportunity to engage and improve in changes.

Having said this, it may be necessary to create new posts in order to carry out the improvements required and many existing staff may be well-suited and qualified to fulfil these posts. What's more, providing new opportunities to existing staff may help motivate and energise them.

In order to overcome any potential barriers to this process it's important that the headteacher/principal and senior team solicit the support of professional associations from the outset. When a teaching union has an opportunity to participate as an active partner in a school's improvement efforts, it is usually easier to create workarounds or renegotiate certain stipulations in teachers' contracts.

Another potential barrier is recruitment, particularly for small rural schools and schools in coastal towns where supply might not meet demand. It's important that headteachers/principals try to combat this (or at least reduce its impact) by developing systems to 'grow their own' future teachers and leaders by encouraging effective teaching assistants to sign up for teacher-training and gain QTS, and by encouraging high-performing teachers to engage in leadership opportunities, perhaps by creating 'associate SLT' positions to work on a short-term project.

*

Now let's examine four common characteristics shared by many of the most successful 'turnaround' schools:

1. Leaders at successful schools make a clear commitment to dramatic changes from the status quo and signal the magnitude and urgency of those changes. Leadership is key, but leaders know that leadership alone is not enough. Instead, leaders also show that dramatic changes are necessary to turn the school around.

2. Turnaround schools focus on improving the quality of teaching at every step of the reform process. To do this, they use data to set goals for instructional improvement, make changes to affect instruction immediately and directly, and continually reassess student learning and instructional practices to refocus the goals.

3. Quick wins (visible improvements early in the turnaround process) are used to rally staff around the effort and overcome resistance and inertia. Certain outcomes that matter to the school result from changes made quickly at senior and middle leadership levels without needing teacher buy-in or approval from outside the school gates, whether that be the local authority, academy trust board or central government and its agencies. Although these initial changes may not improve student achievement immediately, they do set the tone for change. A short-term focus on quick wins establishes a climate for long-term change. Senior leaders may at times feel that they face insurmountable chaos. But when they identify one or two clear goals that can be accomplished quickly, the positive results show that it is possible to reach a school's overarching goal of raising student achievement. It is important for these schools to identify issues that can be addressed quickly and with noticeable success.

4. Senior leaders build a staff that is committed to the school's improvement goals and qualified to meet them. Changes in staff may be required, such as releasing, replacing, or redeploying those who are not fully committed to turning around school performance or bringing in new staff to better meet the goals. Some teachers may retreat to their classrooms to avoid the larger, perhaps negative, school climate. Breaking this pattern may require changes in staff or in the ways that some staff are used. But leaders must focus on having the right staff in the right places. Professional development should be used to help staff reach the school's goals.

In summary, in order to develop the four characteristics shared by successful 'turnaround' schools, it is necessary for schools and their leaders to:

1. Signal a change in leadership practices in the school.
This means making senior leaders into 'instructional leaders' or lead teachers, highly visible in corridors and classrooms. It also means publicly announcing changes and their anticipated actions.

2. Examine data on student achievement to identify specific gaps in student learning.
This means ensuring all teachers use formative data about individual students to analyse their teaching. It also means establishing one or two priority areas for teaching and learning improvement, and making necessary changes in those areas to strengthen teaching and improve student learning. Leaders may plan and deliver targeted professional development based on this analysis of achievement and teaching, differentiated according to teacher needs and the subject areas targeted for instructional improvement. Leaders may also require staff to collaboratively conduct a comprehensive curriculum review aimed at ensuring that the school curriculum aligns with national and local standards, as well as meets the needs of all students in the school. And leaders may insist that all staff regularly monitor progress, and systematically make adjustments to strengthen teaching and student learning and progress.

3. Start with a goal that is important, can be achieved quickly, and will provide visible improvement.
This means developing a strategy for accomplishing the goal that can be implemented quickly. It means considering some common goals for quick wins, such as changing the school's use of time, improving access to resources and the physical facilities, and improving discipline.

4. Assess the strengths and weaknesses of the staff and identify staff who are not fully committed to the school turnaround goals or who do not have the qualifications to carry them out.
This means redeploying staff members who have valuable skills but are not effective in their current role. It could also require replacing staff members who actively resist the school's improvement efforts, then recruiting new staff who have the skills and competencies that are needed for positions in the school.

CHAPTER SEVEN
What does it take to be a 'good' school?

In the previous chapter we looked at ways of transforming inadequate schools. In this chapter we will travel the next leg of the school improvement journey - from 'requires improvement' to 'good'.

The secret of 'getting to good' is investing in a school's most precious (and costly) resource: its people.

Getting to good is about giving teachers the skills and knowledge they need in order to do their jobs well, then continuing to support them and develop their skills, knowledge and experience. Getting to good is about developing systems of collaboration so that professional development becomes an everyday collective exercise not an end of year 'sheep dip'. Getting to good is about individualising professional development, too, so that it is made meaningful and encompasses all forms of professional development such as reading research papers, books, blogs and social media, not just sleeping through a generic training course.

The secret of 'getting to good' is also about ensuring that performance management recognises hard work in all its forms and regards movement up the pay scale as 'the norm', and encourages rather than stifles collaboration instead of promoting competition.

In short, the secret of 'getting to good' is promoting fairness and professionalism; it's building a mature, adult culture in which teachers and leaders work together in the best interests of students to improve the quality of teaching without fear or favour.

But where to start? Here are seven steps to a 'good'...

7 steps to 'good'

1. Remember your core business and always put your learners first

1. Remember your core business and always put your students first

It's important to place your students at the heart of your school and insist on excellence for every student, every day. Never forget that teaching and learning is your core business. Keep students centre-stage by holding regular forums, by asking members of the student council or class representatives to shadow the senior team and attend meetings, and by asking your governors to carry out learning walks.

Have a robust assessment and tracking system in place and ensure that all your students are set aspirational targets at the start of each year. These targets should inform teaching, and students' progress against them should be formally reviewed on a regular basis and this should leading to formative feedback that helps students to make further progress.

Make sure the assessments contained in the tracking system are realistic, challenging and require students to demonstrate a wide range of skills, then support students to achieve greater autonomy in their learning through peer- and self-assessment, and through the use of metacognition and self-regulation.

Ensure that middle and senior leaders know the percentage of students who have received an update against target and the percentage on or above their targets at any one time. Ensure that all those students falling short of expected progress are identified in a timely manner and are supported to improve. Make sure your tracking system monitors the progress of different groups of students so you can put intervention strategies in place to address any concerns. Don't leave it until the end of the year to evaluate and report on attainment gaps - find them early and act quickly to close them.

Support students' development of English and maths by introducing a policy for the marking of cross-curricular literacy, a policy which helps teachers develop consistent strategies for marking spelling, punctuation and grammar, and introduces a set of common marking symbols which students understand. Ensure any student identified as being 'at risk' of underachieving in English and/or maths is referred for support and their progress is tracked. Ensure all supported students have access to small group or one-to-one drop-in workshops or tuition.

Always remember why you do what you do: to prepare students for their next stage of education and, eventually, for the world of work and to be able to participate in society. Maintain an unrelenting focus on developing the skills students need for progression to their next step, including employability and citizenship skills.

7 steps to 'good'

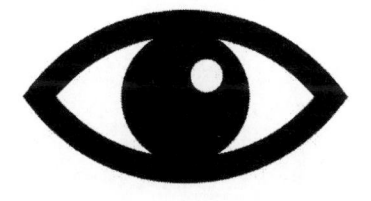

2. Have a clear vision, stick to your strategy, and keep communicating

2. Have a clear vision, stick to your strategy, and keep communicating

Have a clear vision and set of values that articulate where you want the school to be and how you intend to get there. I talked about the importance of vision in Chapter Four so, suffice to say, you need to make sure all the school's stakeholders are afforded the opportunity to consult on the content of the vision and strategy so that they feel involved and invested in the process. Make that vision a reality by writing a strategy which contains a set of common-sense objectives attached to key performance indicators, and a development plan that can be used to report your progress and hold middle and senior leaders to account. Stay focused. Your motto should be: If it isn't in the strategy, it isn't important.

Make sure your vision sets high expectations for students and seeks to achieve a consistency of quality across your school. You shouldn't rest until you know it's not possible for any student to 'fall through the net'.

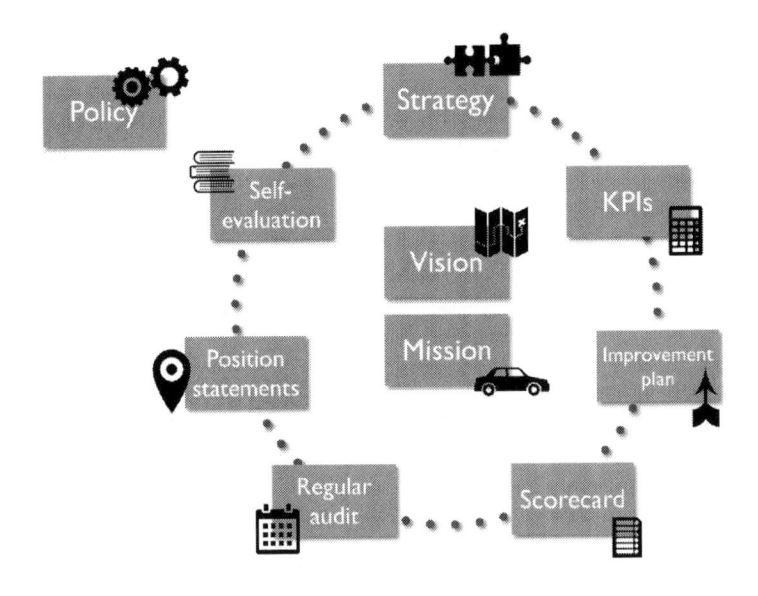

7 steps to 'good'

3. Don't manage performance, develop it

3. Don't manage performance, improve it

In order to achieve consistency, you should move away from the high-stakes, one-off model of performance management and embrace a system of performance improvement. The quality of teaching should be evaluated holistically - for example, by means of a balanced scorecard which aggregates a range of indicators including outcomes for students, target-setting and assessment, lesson planning, student voice, student attendance and punctuality, and professional contributions such as engagement with professional development.

A balanced scorecard isn't just a tool for appraisal, though; it also provides teachers with crucial live data and therefore encourages proactive, student-centric behaviours by highlighting issues and concerns 'as they happen', such as poor attendance and faltering progress.

I'll explore this area in more detail in Chapter Thirteen.

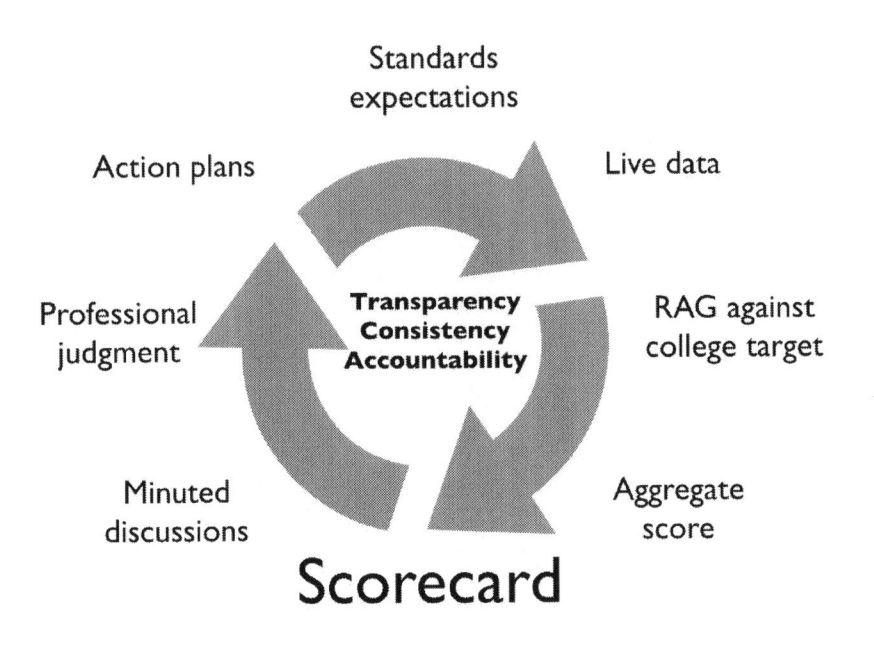

- Standards expectations
- Live data
- RAG against college target
- Aggregate score
- Minuted discussions
- Professional judgment
- Action plans

**Transparency
Consistency
Accountability**

Scorecard

7 steps to 'good'

4. Don't quality assure, quality improve

4. Don't quality assure, quality improve

As well as the balanced scorecard, make sure your quality assurance tools evolve into quality improvement processes - replace stressful and unreliable graded lesson observations with developmental observations that provide every teacher - no matter how good they are - with formative feedback and a SMART action plan for improvement. Complement this with peer observations, coaching, and peer-evaluations of lesson planning materials and marked students' work.

Improve the way your teachers use data to inform their lesson planning and delivery. Provide every teacher with data about each cohort they teach which articulates their students' starting points and individual needs and circumstances which teachers can use to create 'pen portraits' or 'strategic seating plans' to explain how they will meet each student's needs.

7 steps to 'good'

5. Invest in your people and promote collaboration not competition

5. Invest in your people and promote collaboration not competition

As I said earlier, your people are your most costly and precious resource so treasure them. Invest in high-quality professional development and promote the sharing of good practice within and between curriculum departments.

Improve staff induction by making it a year-long programme of support. Ensure all new teachers are assigned a mentor and are given regular access to tailored in-house and external professional development.

Avoid a 'one size fits all' approach to professional development by timetabling weekly sessions for every teacher to be able to access personalised training and share best practice.

Make coaching an entitlement for all teaching staff. Provide teachers with the opportunity to study towards professional qualifications, perhaps part-funded. Allocate time for peer-to-peer support such as co-construction and work scrutiny.

Develop online training solutions and invest in the use of video technology so that professional development can be accessed anytime, anywhere.

Ensure that professional development in all its forms is recognised and celebrated, including reading research papers, books and blogs, and using social media.

I'll explore this in more detail in Chapter Fifteen.

7 steps to 'good'

6. Promote innovation and foster new ideas and approaches

6. Promote innovation and foster new ideas and approaches

In order to enable students to achieve their learning goals between timetabled lessons, invest in appropriate new technologies such as online video hosting which allows staff and students to upload video lectures for flipped learning. Provide all students with email accounts and cloud storage to enable them to work outside of lessons and beyond the school gates, and ensure this replicates workplace practices and therefore supports the development of employability skills.

Link up with other schools and learn from them: increasingly, schools have to deliver more for less but partnering with other organisations and sharing ideas will help you understand ways of overcoming these barriers.

Innovate your curriculum: Think boldly and respond to the needs of your students and the local and national economy. Consider how your school can be unique in what it offers and whether you are providing the skills and qualifications that people in your area need.

7 steps to 'good'

7. Involve, don't just inform, your stakeholders

7. Involve, don't just inform, your governors

Gone are the days when governors could sit passively in the boardroom as senior leaders read their latest headline report. Governors not only need to know far more detail about their school than before, they also need to be much more hands-on. They should work productively with middle and senior leaders to support the school's development and, particularly, improvements in teaching, learning and assessment including through the use of curriculum links and by carrying our learning walks.

Tiered Year-Long Induction
Tailored support for those: 1 New to teaching; 2 New to teaching in schools; 3 New to this school

Weekly CPD
provide opportunity for teams to share best practice, and access tailored training

Learner Voice
surveys and forums to monitor progress; student council involvement in meetings

Standard Expectations
make clear the fundamental, non-negotiable requirements of a teacher

Scorecard
Scorecard informs objective-setting, personal development plans, and appraisals

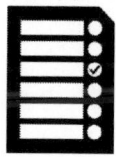

provides holistic evaluation of teacher performance and quality of provision

All teachers use the same system for target-setting, assessment and feedback = **one source of data**

Learning Walks
provide individual developmental feedback and inform departmental and whole-school priorities for improvement

Work Scrutiny
provide feedback on quality and frequency of marking and feedback

Lesson Planning Audits
ensure compliance with whole-school planning expectations

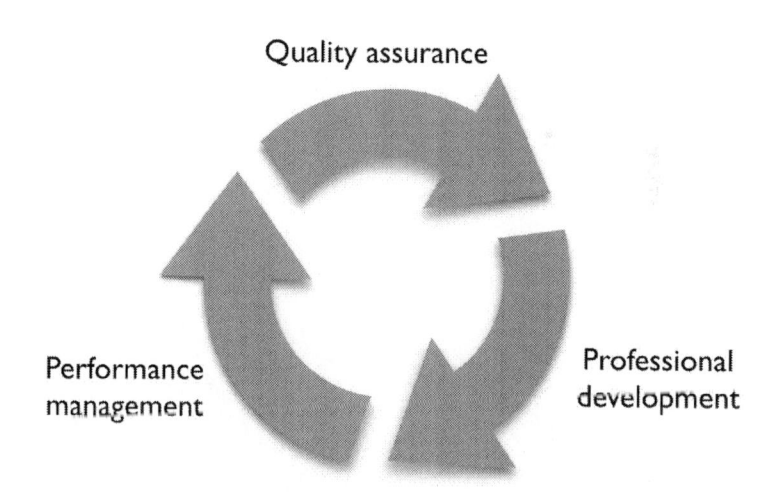

Quality assurance

Performance management

Professional development

CHAPTER EIGHT
What do 'outstanding' schools look like?

So far in this book we have considered the importance of leaders, rather than managers, leading the change effort because leaders have strategic vision (they are able to see clearly where they and their school are going, aim high and share their passion and determination with others, and communicate their plans with enthusiasm and clarity) and strategic planning (they know where their school is now, where they want to go and how they're going to get there).

Leaders know that talk isn't cheap. They know that communication is the key to success because staff need to feel informed and involved in the process of improvement. Leaders know they should be open and honest with colleagues and should seek to reach agreement where possible but should not be afraid to make difficult – perhaps unpopular – decisions when this is right for the school.

Leaders also know that they must not abdicate responsibility but should share it. Where a decision is taken which is not consensual, the rationale should be clearly explained and staff should understand the benefits of that decision for the school and its students.

Leaders do not see it as a weakness to ask for help or advice from colleagues or others; nor are they afraid to admit when they get it wrong. They know that it is a strength, not a weakness, to be self-aware and pragmatic, to adapt to changing circumstances and respond to evolving situations.

Leaders also know that they will achieve genuine, sustainable improvements by tweaking not transforming. They accept that change is uncomfortable and unsettling and that people are not at their best when experiencing change.

Leaders know it is important to understand the status quo, to know what works well and what should be protected and retained. They know that it is important to identify the foundations on which to build because change needs to be incremental; the future needs to be built on the foundations of the past.

So far in this book we have also explored ways of transforming failing schools. We said that there are four ways of turning around an underperforming school in a relatively short space of time, whilst also laying down firm foundations for sustainable improvements. These are as follows:

1. Change school leadership practices,
2. Use data to improve teaching and learning,
3. Achieve 'quick wins' to motivate staff,
4. Achieve a staff consensus and develop leadership capacity.

In the schools which successfully turn themselves around, leaders make a clear commitment to dramatic changes from the status quo and signal the magnitude and urgency of those changes. These schools focus on improving the quality of teaching at every step of the reform process. Quick wins are used to rally staff around the effort and overcome resistance and inertia. And senior leaders build a staff that is committed to the school's improvement goals and qualified to meet them.

Having explored the journey from 'inadequate' to 'requires improvement', we then considered how to get to 'good'. This leg of the school improvement journey, we said, is about giving teachers the skills and knowledge they need in order to do their jobs well, then continuing to support them and develop their skills, knowledge and experience; it's about developing systems of collaboration so that professional development becomes an everyday collective exercise not an end of year 'sheep dip'. Getting to good is also about individualising professional development so that it is made meaningful and encompasses all forms of professional development such as reading academic research, not just attending training courses.

And so, now, let us traverse the final leg of our school improvement journey - the journey to 'outstanding'. We'll begin our journey by answering the question, What does an outstanding school look like?

Put simply, an outstanding school is a school which boasts all of these ten components:

1. Effective leadership
2. A shared vision
3. Rich data that is acted upon
4. All students make good progress
5. A rich curriculum and extra curricular activities
6. Motivated and supported staff
7. A purposeful environment
8. No student is left behind
9. High levels of challenge and engagement
10. Informed and involved parents and communities

Let's take a closer look at each of these ten features...

1. Effective leadership

1. Effective leadership

To be outstanding, a school needs effective leadership, which is to say leadership that is strong and has a clear direction, and leadership that is inclusive of all staff and students.

2. A shared vision

2. A shared vision

To be outstanding, a school needs a shared vision, a clear idea of where it is headed (a common goal) and how it is going to get there; an outstanding school also needs an effective school improvement plan and effective systems of monitoring and evaluating performance which are understood by all staff.

3. Rich data that is acted upon

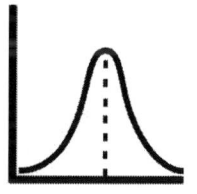

3. Rich data that is acted upon

To be outstanding, a school needs to a workplace in which data is understood by all staff and in which data is used to drive forward improvements, to aid progress and to avoid underachievement.

4. All students make progress

4. All students make progress

To be outstanding, a school needs to be an environment in which all students make good or better progress, and in which students are given aspirational targets. Intervention needs to take place early and be effective and personalised. Student progress needs to be tracked and students need to be rewarded for their hard work.

5. A rich curriculum and a range of extra-curricular activities

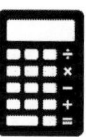

5. A rich curriculum and a range of extra-curricular activities

To be outstanding, a school needs to offer a broad, engaging curriculum which meets the needs of all students and provides a gateway to their future success. What's more, an outstanding school is one in which there is a variety of engaging and appropriate extra-curricular activities which extend the boundaries of learning and provide a safe environment for young people. An outstanding school also provides extra-curricular activities which actively encourage community involvement and participation, and widen students' knowledge and experience.

6. Staff are supported and motivated

6. Motivated and supported staff

To be outstanding, a school's staff need to be well-supported and cared for, and they need to be motivated to work hard and take pride in a job well done. An outstanding school is one in which professional development is taken seriously and staff are valued and have the tools they need to do their jobs.

7. A purposeful environment

7. A purposeful environment

To be outstanding, a school needs to provide a well-organised and attractive environment – an environment which is physically engaging and conducive to learning, as well as metaphysically engaging with effective (i.e. not bureaucratic and not time-consuming) systems and structures.

8. No student is left behind

8. No student is left behind

To be outstanding, a school needs to ensure that vulnerable and disadvantaged children are identified early, their needs are known, and all staff are appropriately trained and have the skills required to support them effectively.

9. High levels of challenge and engagement

9. High levels of challenge and engagement

To be outstanding, a school needs to be a place where all students are challenged by hard work, and actively engaged in their learning. All students need to be encouraged to work hard and to be rewarded for their efforts. Outstanding schools are also places where there are clear, effective sanctions in place.

10. Informed and involved parents and communities

10. Informed and involved parents and communities

To be outstanding, a school needs to give parents a strong voice and it needs to encourage parents to contribute to school life. An outstanding school is also one in which the community and the school work together for the benefit of all. An outstanding school is one in which governors take an active interest in school life, are knowledgeable about what happens in school, and strike the right balance between support and challenge: they are a critical friend working as servants of the school - indeed, acting as ambassadors of the school in the wider community - but are not afraid to question its direction.

CHAPTER NINE
How can leaders run a successful inspection?

Once you've done the real job of improving a school, you'll probably need to convince the schools inspectorate of the fact. To be clear, Ofsted are not why we do what we do as school leaders and teachers; we do what we do for our students. If we're doing all the right things and getting results, we have nothing to fear from an inspection and nothing to gain from providing a 'showcase' - massaging data and inventing paperwork.

However, the process of school inspection is not - no matter how much we wish it was - business as usual...

In a full section 5 inspection, with several inspectors on site for two days demanding several meetings a day, it is impossible for the school leadership team to carry on as if it's just a normal week. The headteacher/principal, for example, is likely to chair staff briefings at 7, be in meetings with inspectors from 8.30 and continue to be in and out of such meetings all day until the final 'keeping in touch' session at 4.30, after which will be the daily staff de-brief at 6. Between the last meeting of the day and the first meeting the following day, there's always more work to be done gathering together and proofing any new information that's just been requested.

An effective base-room is therefore vital to a school's success...

An Ofsted base-room is the beating heart of any school inspection. It is the nerve centre (as well as a centre of nerves); it is the war room from which battles are planned and troops are sent forth to execute those plans; and it is the barracks to which loyal soldiers return, war-weary, to be debriefed and retooled for their next attack.

Get the base-room right, run it like a well-oiled machine and create an atmosphere of calm and positivity, and half the battle will be fought and won.

So what does an effective base room look and feel like? What systems and structures, processes and procedures are needed and how can we ensure an inspection is controlled with military precision?

First of all, it's important to remember that for a majority of school staff an inspection is stressful. The first job for any senior leader, therefore, is to 'walk the floor' as often as possible, be visible, and offer words of encouragement and praise.

The school leadership team's presence in the base-room is important but so is their continued presence outside of it, so they mustn't barricade themselves in, they should plan time to visit every corner of the school site. Projecting calm and confidence might mean acting - portraying the swan effortlessly gliding across the water's surface no matter how frantically the legs are pedalling beneath - but people need to feel like they're in safe hands and leadership means leading by example and leading from the front.

The inside of the base-room should also exude this sense of calm collectedness. It should provide a safe space for colleagues to seek help and advice, to offload their stresses and strains. More than anything, though, the base-room should be organised and purposeful.

Preparing the headteacher/principal's briefing

It's likely that the lead inspector will wish to meet with the headteacher/principal at the start of the first day of inspection to discuss their pre-inspection briefing and agree the format of the next two days. This is an opportunity for the headteacher/principal to articulate their view of their school, to set the tone. This 'state of the nation' address needs to be kept brief, however. The headteacher/principal should skip the detailed narrative around the school's 'unique' context and challenges, which are often seen as excuses for poor performance, and instead stick to the headlines which might include:

• What improvements have been implemented since the last inspection or within the last one-to-three years, and what has been their impact on outcomes;
• What does last year's outcomes data and this year's progress and predictions data look like and why?;
• What are the school's vision, mission and strategy and how do these penetrate the organisation in order to drive improvements?;

- How are senior leaders held to account by governors, including through the use of KPIs?;
- How are middle managers held to account by the senior leadership team?;
- How are teachers held to account by their managers and how does the accountability system ensure fairness and trust?
- What are the procedures for performance management and professional development and what has been their impact?;
- What are students and parents saying about the school?

Prepare colleagues for meetings

Preparing colleagues for meetings

Most staff will welcome some words of encouragement immediately prior to meeting with inspectors and will be eager for advice. But a pre-meeting briefing should avoid exacerbating people's natural stress by posing more questions than it answers. Run through a series of probable questions but try to issue these in advance and allow colleagues time to think through their responses. Provide colleagues with a framework for answering inspectors' questions, which may follow the students' journey, and some key lines of attack. Above all, instil confidence, remind colleagues they have nothing to worry about because they've been doing a great job and are fully prepared.

De-brief colleagues after meetings

De-briefing colleagues after meetings

It's important that colleagues feed back as early as possible following a meeting with inspectors. They need the conversation fresh in their memories so they can input into the system the questions they were asked and what further information or follow-up activity inspectors requested. Positivity is again key to the success of this meeting: staff need to feel valued as part of the inspection process and you need them walking out smiling.

Prepare position statements and other documentation

Preparing position statements and other documentation

Although Ofsted should accept whatever documentation and in whatever form the school ordinarily uses, it will be necessary to produce some position papers and data summaries for the purposes of inspection. Often, colleagues will emerge from their meetings with inspectors with a list of requests.

It is not uncommon for more than one inspector to request the same information so keeping a central record of who has asked for what and by when is vital to ensuring a consistent approach and to avoiding unnecessary duplication.

It is the responsibility of whoever is running the base-room to ensure that every document that's handed to inspectors is proofed for accuracy and consistency first. Nothing should leave the room without it being checked for spelling, punctuation and grammar, and without all the data contained within it being validated. If two documents make it into inspectors' hands with contradictory data, the job of convincing them you know your provision and can accurately self-evaluate suddenly becomes a lot more difficult.

It may be necessary to proof and redact copies of key documentation prior to the start of the inspection so that these are made available on the first day or uploaded to the portal. It is likely you'll be asked for samples of minutes from all key meetings and other evidence of your systems at work including performance management and appraisals, records of professional development activity and their impact, the school vision and mission, and the school improvement plan and self-evaluation form. It is helpful to have samples of these documents from various levels of the hierarchy including at subject level. This shows your systems pervade the organisation and everyone is working together, headed in the same direction. Consistency in all things is key to a successful inspection.

Pick your battles

Pick your battles

When you read the pre-inspection briefing, you might be overcome by the sheer number of 'points to consider' but don't take it personally. It's a starting point, a guide to help the inspection team answer some unanswered questions, dot the i's and cross the t's.

Some of the discussion points will be based on assumptions, some of which will be false. Be quick to correct mistakes, providing supporting evidence, then 'pick your battles'.

It's sometimes wise - and a sign of effective self-evaluation - to accept some criticisms and 'put them to bed' early.

Be frank: you haven't got some things right yet, and some aspects of your performance aren't good enough. What this says is that you know your areas for development and have a plan to address them. You're realists.

Once you've accepted and conceded some points, pick the discussion points that are worth fighting for and about which you know you have strong, robust evidence and narratives. To help, consider which points are likely to influence the overall grading and which may simply fade away as the week of inspection progresses. Fight for the 'grade-changers' but let the small things go. Life's too short.

Impact, impact, impact

Impact, impact, impact

When you say anything, be prepared to point to the impact. In other words, always be ready to answer the 'so what?' question. It might help to frame any points you make as follows:

- In order to...

- We...
- As a result of which...
- We know this because...
- And the impact on students was...
- Our next step is...

Storytelling

In order to exemplify your evidence of improvement, prepare some case studies which put names and faces to the cold, hard data; make the stats come alive.

For example, I'd advise you prepare case studies for the following topics (note that some case studies will serve as exemplars for more than one topic, of course):

- Quality assurance processes
- How you've improved under-performing subjects/teachers
- Performance management
- Professional development
- English and maths (achievement in English and maths lessons but also the success of literacy and numeracy across the curriculum)
- Equality and diversity (the promotion of, and diminishing the differences between, groups of students)
- How students are stretched and challenged to achieve high grades
- How students with special educational needs and disabilities - and other vulnerable or disadvantaged students - are helped to become increasingly independent
- The frequency, quality and content of the information, advice and guidance (IAG) that's given to students throughout their journey through school
- Work experience and enrichment activities
- Managing attendance and punctuality
- Target-setting, assessment and feedback
- Tracking of student progress and timely intervention
- Curriculum development
- How technology is used to extend learning and expedite progress
- Pastoral care and safeguarding
- Promoting fundamental British values, and the Prevent agenda

For each of these case studies, have examples for all types of student.

Get in-year data

In-year data

The further into an academic year your inspection comes, the more important your in-year data will become. You will need to show how you set student targets and how - and how often - you assess their progress against these targets in order to make predictions for outcomes and put in place timely interventions to stretch and challenge higher performing students and scaffold and support the lower-performing.

You will need to ensure your data not only shows achievement against target but also the level of progress made from individual starting points, including value added data (use DfE L3VA predictions as well as ALPs if it's available).

You should also have data showing any achievement gaps or rather how you're diminishing the differences between the achievement of different groups of students. Are there any differences between the levels of progress made by students of different ages, ethnicities, and prior attainment, as well as students with different learning needs including those with a special educational need or disability? In-year data should also cover attendance and punctuality, not just progress.

All in-year data should be compared to the same point the previous year rather than to end-of-year outcomes, so that it is like-for-like. It would be useful to have evidence to support the claim that in-year assessments are accurate - for example, how well did last year's predictions turn out? What systems do you have in place to ensure teacher assessments are moderated and standardised?

Finally, an important point that's often neglected, you should provide evidence that all the data you collect is being used to inform planning and teaching, and to inform curriculum design.

CHAPTER TEN
How can leaders manage change?

Any process of school improvement - whichever leg of the journey you are on - necessarily involves change because, if a school is to improve, it must, by definition, change. Managing change, therefore, is an important skill for school leaders. Many senior leaders enjoy working against a backdrop of continuous change because it makes their jobs interesting, challenging and varied. It gives them a chance to stamp their mark on the organisation, to show what they are capable of. But it's important to remember that not everyone shares this passion for change.

Leaders should start with the knowledge that change can be uncomfortable, particularly for those who feel that change is being done to them not by them. Leaders should also bear in mind that many staff will resent change and will either refuse to engage with it or, worse, act to prevent it from happening. And, as I say above, a school can only become outstanding if everyone works together. So what is the best way to manage change? First, it is important to understand why people are resistant to it...

People are resistant to change because:
- They are anxious of the impact it will have on their jobs
- They feel they have tried it before and it didn't work
- They fear it will mean more work for them
- They do not understand the need for change, they like the status quo
- They fear failure
- They are scared by the pace of change and by being out of their comfort zone
- They fear change will prove too costly or a waste of time and money

People are resistant to change because change implies that the status quo isn't good enough, that the way people work now is in some way inadequate. People also resent change because it signals the destruction of all they have worked hard to achieve. Change means abandoning what they know and what they like. All of these things may be true, of course: the status quo may not be good enough; the way people work now may indeed be inadequate. But it is unlikely your school is so thoroughly broken that it requires a total transformation. It is more likely that there will be lots of things about your school that should be retained, preserved, protected. Even if it is so utterly broken that it needs wholesale change, the process of mending it should be done gradually and with the support of staff: this means careful management, a lot of tact and patience.

Once you understand people's resistance to change, you should begin to engage them in the process of change. As a starting point, it is important to:

Be open and honest about the need for change: involve your staff as early as possible, ideally involve them in the process of identifying the need for change in the first place.

Explain the rationale behind change: on what evidence have you based your decision to change? What do you hope this change will achieve and why is that important?

Outline the benefits of change for everyone: what is it in for staff, students, parents and governors? How will change make their working lives easier and more rewarding?

Senior leaders need to use the following skills when managing change:

1. Patience and self-control
Leaders need to stay calm and considered at all times, and they need to think and behave rationally.

2. Balance
Leaders need to balance the needs of students with the needs of staff, as well as balance the need to improve teaching and learning with the school's financial needs.

3. Communication
Leaders need to keep others informed and involved at all times and ensure communication is genuinely two-way.

4. Problem-solving
Leaders needs to think through the options and find appropriate solutions.

5. Personal ownership

Leaders need to showing initiative and be conscientious; leaders need to take responsibility for their decisions and actions and for the consequences of those decisions and actions.

Leaders of change also need enthusiasm, flexibility, energy and tenacity if they are to succeed in bringing about lasting, positive change which, in turn, leads to genuine and sustainable school improvement.

I find a change management cycle useful in planning for change. The cycle I use is as follows:

1. Mobilise
2. Discover
3. Deepen
4. Develop
5. Deliver

What does the change management cycle mean in practice?

Mobilise

First, it is important to understand why some colleagues may resist change. You need to tackle this head-on by explaining why change is necessary (where is the need, what is the rationale?) and by outlining the benefits of change for everyone involved. Then you need to involve your staff in the process of change: don't let them see change as something being done to them by the senior team, let them feel genuinely a part of the process and able to contribute to it and affect it. A good way to mobilise staff is to establish 'change teams' or working parties which will be the driving force behind change. Change teams should be representative of all staff.

Discover

One of the first jobs for the change team is to identify and acknowledge the issues involved in change. It means developing a deeper understanding of what change will involve and how barriers will be overcome. This might involve members of the change team consulting with others and bringing ideas and issues back to the table. For example, your change team may include a member of each department or faculty, a member of support staff and a teaching assistant. It may include a member of the admin team and/or site staff. Discovering the issues may be as simple as conducting a SWOT analysis or may be more complex.

Deepen

The change team then needs to develop a deeper knowledge and understanding of the scale and scope of the changes that are required. They also need to know and understand the root causes of the issues that led to change being needed in the first place, as well as the issues that will inevitably arise whilst change is being enacted. This stage is about being forewarned and forearmed, about being prepared for the road ahead. It is also about setting the boundaries - knowing what will be included in the project and what will not - and setting appropriate timescales.

Develop

This stage is about suggesting solutions, coming up with improvements to the way people work. It is about the change team taking action, trialling new methods of working and finding out what is effective and what isn't. It is important at this stage to prioritise those actions which will have the biggest impact. Start with a splash not a ripple. You want other staff to see the impact of what you're doing, you want them to see that change is for the better, that you are getting results and making life easier. You want to win over your detractors and those most resistant to change, you want to convince them that what you're doing is right. For example, your change team may trial a new teaching method - let's say the use of daily low-stakes quizzes as a form of retrieval practice - and this may be videoed and played at a faculty meeting or on a training day in order to show all your staff that such an approach works in your school. This may then encourage others to try it out, too.

Deliver

This stage is about making change happen. The change team now rolls out the changes they have developed and refined to the whole school. The plans formed in the 'develop' stage are now fully agreed and everyone begins to implement them, again starting with the high impact actions or 'quick wins'.

*

In summary, effective change requires:

Effective leadership

Effective leadership is democratic, it acts as a role model, it supports and encourages others. Why? Because effective leadership leads to people feeling involved and valued, provides broader, richer insights and ideas, and helps improve staff morale, as well as recruitment and retention; effective leadership also shares responsibility, leads to less stress, higher standards of teaching, effective collaboration and more honest relationships in which problems are aired and resolved faster.

An inclusive culture

An inclusive culture is one in which people know they can contribute and overcome barriers together, in which everyone is encouraged to play a part in driving the school's change agenda.

Broad collaboration

This means collaboration between schools, stakeholders and other organisations which helps embed a culture of openness to positive change.

Change teams

Change teams are working parties which are inclusive and representative of all areas of school, a team which acts as a communication channel between the senior team and the workforce and which makes staff feel involved in their school.

CHAPTER ELEVEN
How can leaders avoid change management mistakes?

In Chapter Ten we looked at how to manage change. But even with the best will in the world and a prevailing wind, mistakes can and will be made, and your best laid schemes will not always go to plan. Some mistakes can be foreseen, however; and thus they can be avoided or mitigated.

In an article for Harvard Business Review in 1995 called Leading Change, John Kotter explained why some attempts to change the way organisations work are unsuccessful.

The first mistake many organisations make when seeking to improve the way they work is to lack a sense of urgency. Effective change requires the aggressive cooperation of many individuals and yet, without motivation, these people will not help and the effort will go nowhere. Many organisations fail to establish a sense of urgency because they worry that their staff will become defensive and that morale will drop. They worry that events will spiral out of control and short-term results will be jeopardised.

A sense of urgency is created when a frank discussion is had about some potentially unpleasant or uncomfortable realities: namely, that the organisation's performance isn't as good as people think it is and/or that the tectonic plates on which the organisation is built, are shifting and sliding at a rapid pace and the organisation is losing its footing. The purpose of such discussions is to make it clear that the status quo is more dangerous than change.

You will know when the sense of urgency is at the right level when over 75% of school staff know that operating on a business-as-usual basis is inadvisable, unacceptable and unsustainable.

The second mistake many organisations make when seeking to improve is failing to create a powerful coalition of senior staff. A successful team might only consist of four or five people in the first phase but it needs to grow quickly before real progress can be made.

A guiding coalition develops a shared commitment to improving performance through change. Although not every senior member of staff will buy into the transformation effort to begin with, the coalition must be appropriately powerful in terms of job titles and status, reputations and relationships in order to affect change.

The third mistake is lacking a clear vision – the most successful guiding coalitions develop an image of the future that is easy to communicate and appeals to all its organisation's stakeholders. The vision clearly articulates the direction of travel the organisation will take in order to become successful. Often the first draft of the vision comes from an individual who drives change but it is later refined by many others.

Without a clear and positive vision for the future of the organisation, impetus can be lost and the purpose of change can become muddy and confused. A successful vision can be communicated in less than five minutes and can garner a reaction that shows that the audience both understand it and are interested in working towards it.

The fourth mistake is not communicating the vision effectively enough or frequently enough. Without a lot of effective communication, hearts and minds cannot be won. And the vision must be communicated repeatedly, it must be incorporated into everything the organisation says and does. Emails, newsletters, staff meetings, and appraisals are all focused on articulating and achieving the vision.

The vision is communicated in both words and actions, too: no one's behaviour must undermine the vision and senior staff must behave in a way that is wholly consistent with the vision.

The fifth mistake is failing to remove the barriers that stand in the way of achieving the vision. Although senior staff can empower others to take action simply by communicating the vision, this is not enough on its own. Instead, effective change requires the removal of any barriers to change.

Often, a member of staff understands and agrees with the vision but is prevented from helping to achieve it because there is a road block in their way. Sometimes this block is a process and sometimes it is a person. Sometimes people are fearful for their jobs, and/or appraisal systems make them act out of self-interest rather than in the best interests of the organisation.

The guiding coalition, therefore, need to understand what the barriers to their vision are and then actively work to remove them – this might mean changing policies and procedures and it might mean removing some rogue staff.

The sixth mistake is failing to plan for and create 'quick wins'. Most people need compelling evidence that change will be successful within a year or less before they will commit to it. Creating short-term 'wins', therefore, is important as a means of motivating staff and convincing them that change will work.

Creating quick wins is not the same as simply hoping for a win – a successful transformation effort involves leaders actively seeking out ways of improving performance. They establish short-term goals that act as checkpoints on the journey towards achieving the long-term vision, and they work hard to ensure that those goals are scored and, once they are scored, they reward their staff accordingly.

The seventh mistake is to declare victory too soon. It is good to set short-term goals along the way and to celebrate when you achieve them – but never forget that these are small battles in a much bigger war. It is important not to declare the war to be won too soon. Instead, use the credibility afforded by achieving short-term goals as a means of tackling the bigger issues. Start work on abolishing systems and structures that are inconsistent with the vision or that stand in the way of achieving that vision.

The final mistake is failing to reconcile the new vision with the organisation's established culture. Transformation is only successful and sustainable when it becomes the norm, the accepted culture, 'the way we do things around here'.

The vision has to become the expected and established way of working. There are two key factors to consider here:

Firstly, you need to signpost for staff how the new ways of working have explicitly led to improvements, make clear that the changes you've introduced have been successful in achieving a better performance. If you are not explicit about this, people are likely to make different connections or no connections at all. Communication is the key here: tell a story linking your vision and your changes to the successes you're subsequently enjoying, and tell that story relentlessly. Dedicate meetings and emails to explaining how success was achieved.

Secondly, you need to make sure that any new appointments, particularly new leaders and managers, are well matched to the vision and model the behaviours you need. A poor appointment at a senior level can undermine the vision and the transformation you have worked hard to achieve.

In conclusion, if we are to learn from these common mistakes, we should infer that an effective change management process - as well as following a cycle such as the one I set out in the previous chapter - follows these eight steps:

1. Establishing a sense of urgency
2. Forming a powerful guiding coalition
3. Creating a vision
4. Communicating the vision
5. Empowering others to act on the vision
6. Planning for and creating short-term wins
7. Consolidating improvements and producing still more change
8. Institutionalising new approaches

CHAPTER TWELVE
How can leaders manage conflict?

I've already argued that an effective leader is:

- a good listener; able to care about and respond to people's needs
- consistent, fair and honest; transparent and above reproach
- sensitive, able to show warmth and to empathise with people's concerns and worries
- able to give quality time to people, be available and approachable
- able to show assertiveness, determination and strength of response, yet be kind and calm and courageous
- able to communicate - through a variety of means and in an appropriate manner - with enthusiasm, passion and drive.

But, above all these things, I said, a good leader is a human being.

As human beings, leaders are controlled by their instincts. In fact, in every human brain there is a constant battle between the frontal cortex and the limbic system. The frontal cortex is the rational side; the limbic system is irrational. The limbic system has been called 'the chimp' because it is the primitive part of our brain and often tries to control our actions with pure, naked instincts. It asks 'how do I feel?' rather than 'what do I think?' Or 'what is logical?' and seeks an emotional fight or flight response to conflict. The frontal cortex, meanwhile, is the rational side which is concerned with thoughts rather than feelings.

Unfortunately, the limbic system - because it works on instinct - is faster to act than the frontal cortex which takes time to consider what is logical and rational under the circumstances and seeks to place events in context. This is why there is a constant war being waged in our heads. Our frontal cortex is always trying to wrest back control from the limbic system. Let me give you an example…

I engage in public speaking all the time. Indeed, it's my bread and butter these days. But, no matter how often I stand up in front of a large audience, I still feel nervous beforehand. I don't mind this. In fact, the day I no longer feel nervous is the day I stop because nervousness means I produce lots of adrenaline and adrenaline makes me alert and helps me to perform better. But when I'm in the spotlight, immediately before I speak, my frontal cortex is doing battle with my limbic system in an internal power struggle. My limbic system is telling me I'm rubbish, I'm unprepared, can't remember a word of what I'm due to say, and that the audience doesn't respect me and is going to be a tough crowd. My frontal cortex, meanwhile, is trying to be rational and stop my limbic system from taking control. It reminds me that I'm prepared and have rehearsed, that the audience will be willing me to do well and will forgive - or not notice - any minor mis-steps I make.

Whenever we face conflict, our frontal cortex and our limbic system do battle in this way. The chimp goes into fight or flight mode and makes us emotional and irrational. It gets our blood pumping, our heart racing and our dander up! But this is the worst possible way to respond to conflict. It's important, therefore, to acknowledge the chimp's existence and be mindful of how it's trying to shape our response. And then we need to put the chimp back in its box and allow our frontal cortex to take control and provide a logical, rational response that stands up to scrutiny.

*

As I've already said, above all, good leaders are human beings because they care about other people's feelings, are empathetic, and give time and support to people when they need it most. But because they're human they are also controlled by their feelings and are, therefore, fallible and imperfect. Sometimes they will make mistakes. What's important is that they acknowledge their mistakes and seek to make amends. And, moreover, what's important is that they work hard to avoid making the same mistakes again by wresting control of their chimp.

The best way to take control of the limbic system is to mentally compartmentalise the personal from the professional. Conflict in the workplace is never - or at least very rarely - personal. In the workplace I have never raised my voice at a colleague and indeed, as a teacher and headteacher, hardly ever did so with students. I model patience and diplomacy. At home, however, I often lose my temper with my children and - let me whisper this confidentially - have even been known to shout!

That's because my home life is personal and my work life is professional. I separate them cleanly in my mind. Whenever I face conflict at work, I remind myself it isn't personal and that I must be professional. If I lose my patience I have lost the argument and some moral standing.

So how can we control our emotions, remain professional, and either prevent conflict or deal with it effectively when it arises?

One answer is to start with the self: analyse ourselves in order to become more self-aware. Developing a sense of emotional intelligence is one way to do this. Daniel Goleman developed a three-step model of emotional intelligence:

1. Know yourself (what he called self-mastery)
2. Know others (what he called social radar), and
3. Control your response.

According to Weare (2004), emotional intelligence is "the ability to understand ourselves and other people, and in particular to be aware of, understand and use information about the emotional states of ourselves and others with competence. It includes the ability to understand, express and manage our own emotions, and respond to the emotions of others, in ways that are helpful to ourselves and others."

Goleman posited five skill domains that are particularly pertinent to school leadership:

1. Self awareness
2. Managing feelings
3. Motivation
4. Empathy
5. Social skills

Emotional intelligence allows us to model the sorts of behavioural responses we expect to see from others. This is no more important than when dealing with difficult people. If we don't model the desired behaviours then we cannot expect these difficult people to mirror them and to behave more appropriately towards us. We also need to be aware of our own ongoing emotional state and conduct a realistic assessment of our own strengths and weaknesses. We need to be aware of the emotional state of our colleagues, too, and deploy appropriate and measured responses - in a calm and considered way - in what can be highly charged emotional situations.

To be confident of accurately self-assessing, we need to be aware of our strengths and weaknesses, we need to be reflective and learn from our experiences, and we need to be open to candid feedback, to new perspectives, and to continuous learning and self-development.

To be self-confident, we need to present ourselves with self-assurance, we need presence, we need to be able to voice our views even if those views may be unpopular, we need to be willing to fight for what we believe and for what is right, and we need to be decisive, able to make sound decisions despite uncertainties and external pressures.

To be emotionally aware, we need to know which emotions we are feeling and why, realise the links between our feelings and what we think, do and say, recognise how our feelings affect our performance, and never lose sight of our values and goals.

When confronted with difficult people or difficult situations, it is common to seek to avoid conflict or to deny that conflict exists. We may wait until conflict goes away or we may try to change the subject. It is also common, when accepting that conflict exists, to react emotionally, to become aggressive, abusive, or even hysterical. It is common, too, to find someone else to blame for conflict, to make excuses or to let someone else deal with it. But avoiding or denying conflict will only exacerbate the situation and make us look like weak leaders.

Leaders do not deny conflict; they deal with it and do so effectively…

In dealing with conflict, we need to remember that it is a process not a singular event. In other words, conflict is not - or is rarely - a one-off occurrence that has emerged out of nowhere and will dissipate just as quickly. Rather, conflict builds over time. There is, if we look back, a road that led to conflict and, broadly speaking, there are five pit-stops along the road to breakdown:

1. Discussion
2. Debate
3. Argument
4. Conflict
5. Breakdown

Let's take a look at each in turn…

1. Discussion
This is when both people are interested in the other's view of the world and are prepared to share ideas, opinions and feelings. This stage is simply a meeting of minds with no intention to get the other person to think or feel anything different. Discussion is usually characterised by a respect for each other's viewpoint, an acceptance of the other's values, and a broadening of perspectives.

2. Debate
This is when there are different viewpoints and one person would like the other to see things their way, but only if it is right for them. This stage is usually characterised by an openness to each other's ideas and by a respect for the other's viewpoint.

3. Argument
At this stage, one person wants the other to 'buy' their ideas, regardless of what they may be thinking. One person believes they are 'right' and the other person is 'wrong'. The other person should be doing it their way. This stage is characterised by a disregard for the other's viewpoint, by arguing from one perspective only and therefore a polarisation of opinions, and by the use of lots of "yes... buts".

4. Conflict
At this stage, not only does one person believe they are 'right' and the other person is 'wrong' but that person insists they do it their way, that the other person acts according to their values and beliefs. Conflict is characterised by demands that "you behave as I want you to", by increasingly personalised arguments and the use of lots of "shoulds", as well as by blame, accusation, and put-downs.

5. Breakdown
At this stage the dynamic is so difficult that each person involved feels the need to protect themselves or distance themselves in order to recover from confrontation. One person may act as if the other no longer exists or matters. There may be silence or disdain.

This 'road to breakdown' is characterised by a desire for one person to change the other, or by one person blaming the other. However, as school leaders dealing with conflict in the workplace we should remember that trying to change someone rarely results in change. Change is more likely to come about from understanding. Wanting to change someone implies there is something wrong with that person and, naturally, this only leads to them becoming defensive and argumentative. Seeking to understand, however, suggests the other person's point of view is valid and reasonable. This is the approach that creates collaboration and mutual problem-solving.

What's more, as school leaders, we should remember that trying to blame someone is reactive and looks to the past in an attempt to discern who was right and who was wrong. A better approach if our goal is a resolution that allows is to move forwards is to focus on the future and on how the situation can be resolved. This is the difference between arguing who left the stable door open after the horse has bolted, and going out to try find the horse! One approach is reactive, futile and damaging; the other is proactive and solution-focused.

Sometimes, no matter how honourable our intentions and no matter how well we deal with conflict, we will encounter someone who is angry and whose anger is expressed inappropriately. In order to disarm that anger, we should listen to what they have to say and stay silent if necessary. This will allow them a right of reply and enable them to vent their anger. They may simply burn out and feel better for having said what they needed to say.

Throughout an angry exchange, we should maintain rapport in both body and voice. We should try to feed back what we hear. It may be possible to change what the person is focused on by asking questions. We should certainly attempt to make empathetic statements that show we understand even if we disagree. Being empathetic is not the same as agreeing with their point of view or saying they are right. When feeding back what the person has said, it may be helpful to take notes and to number their concerns as a list to be acted upon. Feeding back what we think the person has said, and asking them to confirm or clarify if we've understood correctly, helps move the conversation towards action and is much more solution orientated than simply sitting silent,y and impassively, and certainly more helpful than arguing back.

Another useful strategy to employ when dealing with angry people is to use bridging language rather than barrier language. Conflict can be escalated or defused depending on the way we respond to it. People react to what we say and do, so whether we attack or defend, advance or retreat, anger or appease, we affect how the other person responds. What starts as a discussion can escalate without proper management.

Firstly, we should not avoid conflict and anger. That may simply escalate the situation. Secondly, we should avoid being defensive - it is rarely personal. Thirdly, we should avoid over-generalising about how someone feels and why they feel that way. Fourthly, we should listen and seek to understand the person's point of view. Fifthly, we should remember that we don't have to 'win'. What matters is that communication channels remain open.

A 'barrier' mindset, then, is characterised by the following attitudes:
- I am right
- You should change
- You are the problem
- I want power over you
- I want to lay down the law
- I want to prove you wrong
- I am indifferent to your needs
- You are wrong and you should be different
- My needs are more important than yours

These attitudes are often articulated by using the following words and phrases:
- Me
- You should
- Waste of time
- Your problem is
- That won't work
- Out of the question
- That's my final word
- This is non-negotiable
- You don't understand
- I've heard all this before
- You wouldn't understand

And by the following actions:
- Frowning
- Lip-biting
- Raised voice
- Arms crossed
- Hands on hips
- Sharp gestures
- Hands in pockets
- Hands over mouth
- Avoiding eye contact
- Narrowing of the eyes

A 'bridging' mindset, by contrast, is characterised by the following attitudes:

- You are OK
- Let's work together
- I want us both to win
- I want power with you
- Your needs are important
- Let's problem-solve rather than argue
- We have a mutual problem to be solved

And these attitudes are often articulated via the frequent use of the following words and phrases:

- Us
- We
- Our
- Can
- Let's talk
- Appreciate
- Alternatives
- What do you need?
- What do you think?
- Help me understand
- What would you say to...?

...and through the following actions:
- Open posture
- Eye contact
- Low and slow voice
- Looking and acting approachable
- Sitting or standing at an angle of approximately 90°
- Using open hand gestures – palms slightly upturned

When confronted with difficult people, I try to remember to sail on a calm SEA which means I stay in control of:
- The **situation** by putting clear boundaries in place,
- My **emotions** by staying calm and professional, thus giving myself the confidence to face whatever problem comes my way, and
- The **action** I plan to take, moving the discussion forward.

When a situation calls for more assertive action, I remember to make eye contact in order to indicate interest and sincerity. I remember to take care of my body posture which can be used to emphasise what I am saying. I remember gestures which can also give emphasis to what I am saying. I remember my voice, using the tone and timbre to convince rather than dominate or intimidate. And I remember the golden rules of listening which are:

- Give the other person your undivided attention. Don't do other work or take calls while you are listening.
- Find a quiet place to listen. Avoid places that are noisy or have other distractions.
- Listen to be influenced. Don't allow your mind to be distracted with trying to think up rebuttals.
- Don't interrupt. Let people finish their point.
- Show that you are interested. Do this by nodding or saying "yes" or "ah ha".
- Maintain eye contact without staring.
- Look at the person – use eye contact and an open posture

To conclude, here are my top ten strategies for managing conflict and dealing with difficult people:

1. Listen: Say nothing; don't interrupt; don't hurry. Then listen some more.
2. Empathise: Put yourself in the other person's shoes; validate their feelings.
3. De-personalise: Put your feelings to one side - it's not about you.
4. Be informed: Know how (understand school policies and procedures) and who (understand school staff roles and responsibilities).
5. Defuse or decamp: Apply calming techniques or remove yourself from harm.
6. Focus: Keep the resolution (or the student) at the centre of conversation.
7. Take responsibility: You're not to blame but you are responsible. Say you'll take responsibility and you'll resolve it.
8. Apologise
9. Resolve: Seek quick resolutions and explain them and their timescales.
10. Communication: Keep the other person 'in the loop'; follow up on promises.

CHAPTER THIRTEEN
How can leaders manage teachers' performance?

Once upon a time, not so long ago, teachers were judged by means of a single digit which graded an hour's performance, observed through the narrow lens of one lesson, with one class, and with the biased eyes of one observer. Tell your children that and they won't believe you. 'But that's ridiculous,' they'll protest, 'Surely no one thought that made any sense?' And the answer, of course, is the secret hidden in plain sight, the elephant in the room: it didn't.

If your school is still grading lesson observations and using this score as a proxy for quality assurance and performance management, then you have my deepest sympathies and urgent request that you enact change. I'm confident, though, that the tide has finally turned and school leaders are developing more robust, accurate and - above all - fair systems of performance management and appraisal. I'm not quite so confident, however, that most schools have yet discovered a workable alternative.

When it comes to performance management, my philosophy is simple: it is no one's vocation to fail. In other words, no one wakes up in the morning determined to do the worst job they possibly can; no one opens their eyes, stretches and yawns, looks themselves up and down in the mirror and vows to fail as many students as they can before nightfall. But, despite the best of intentions, sometimes some people don't perform as well as we'd like.

When teachers under-perform, they need to be given time and support – including training – in order to improve. Many will. But those who don't need to leave the profession. Retaining people who cannot perform the duties for which they are paid serves no one well, least of all our students. Accountability – when managed fairly and accurately, honestly and transparently – is a good thing. It ensures the best people do the best jobs; it ensures the teaching profession – and our next generation – is kept safe.

Arguing against ineffective systems of performance management (such as lesson observations) is not - therefore - akin to arguing against the need for accountability. Indeed, performance management matters and it is important school leaders get it right in order to help teachers improve, to reward hard work and challenge persistent underperformance.

A system of accountability based on lesson observations alone - or indeed any single measure - is a broken one because lesson observations do not accurately or reliably measure the quality of teaching nor the effectiveness of teachers. What they do, however, is create a climate of fear; they straitjacket teachers. As a result of high-stakes lesson observations, teachers tend to do one of two things:

1. They over-plan, over-teach and proffer showcase lessons which bear no relation to their everyday practice.

2. They become stressed by the experience of being watched and so under-perform.

In short, high-stakes lesson observations - or any other single-source evaluation tool - do not allow observers to see the teacher as they would normally teach. But even if a teacher is brave enough to teach a 'normal' lesson and does not succumb to the natural stress of observation, the very presence of an observer in the room inevitably alters the classroom dynamics. This is called the Hawthorne Effect.

So what's the answer?

First of all, let me be clear: I'm not suggesting we stop observing lessons altogether. In fact, I think walking into lessons to see what's happening is important. By observing the classroom environment, for example, we can see the rapport the teacher has established with students, we can see how well the teacher manages behaviour and utilises resources. Lesson observations also allow us to see the ways in which transitions are handled and tasks are organised. But observations alone do not enable us to accurately judge the quality of teaching. For that we need to triangulate what we see and hear in classrooms with other sources of information, not least our – much maligned but absolutely vital – professional judgment.

In other words, we should measure the quality of teaching in a holistic not isolated way.

The Measures of Effective Teaching (MET) project by the Bill and Melinda

Gates Foundation was a three-year study which sought to determine how best to identify and promote great teaching. The project concluded that it was possible to identify - and therefore measure - great teaching by combining three types of measures, namely:

1. Classroom observations,
2. Student surveys, and
3. Student achievement gains (or outcomes).

The project report said that "Teaching is complex, and great practice takes time, passion, high-quality materials, and tailored feedback designed to help each teacher continuously grow and improve."

The project's report shows that a more balanced approach – one which incorporates multiple measures such as the student survey data and classroom observations – has two important advantages: teacher ratings are less likely to fluctuate from year to year, and the combination is more likely to identify teachers with better outcomes on student assessments.

The report also offered advice on how to improve the validity of lesson observations. It recommended averaging observations from more than one observer: "If we want students to learn more, teachers must become students of their own teaching. They need to see their own teaching in a new light. This is not about accountability. It's about providing the feedback every professional needs to strive towards excellence."

The project claimed we had to learn four lessons if we were to improve our systems of performance management:

Firstly, teachers generally appear to be managing their classrooms well, but are struggling with fundamental instructional skills.

Secondly, classroom observations can give teachers valuable feedback, but are of limited value for predicting future performance.

Thirdly, value-added analysis is more powerful than any other single measure in predicting a teacher's long-term contributions to student success.

And finally, evaluations that combine several strong performance measures will produce the most accurate results.

The solutions to these problems are as follows:

Firstly, we should base teacher evaluations on multiple measures of performance, including data on student academic progress.

Secondly, we should improve classroom observations by making them more frequent and robust.

Thirdly, we should use or modify an existing observation rubric instead of trying to reinvent the wheel.

Fourthly, we should give evaluators the training and ongoing support they need to be successful.

And finally, we should consider using student surveys as a component of teacher evaluation.

In terms of using multiple measures of effectiveness, the project found that using lesson observation alone had a positive correlation with outcomes of just 0.24. Using student surveys alone had a correlation of 0.37. Using value added data was the most accurate with a correlation of 0.69. But combining all three of these measures had a correlation of 0.72, proving yet again that using multiple measures of performance - measuring teacher effectiveness holistically - is the best solution.

So, if we accept that teaching is a highly complex job, what aspects of it should we measure? What elements of teaching matter most to us and lead to the most significant academic gains for students and, perhaps more pertinently, what elements of teaching can actually be observed and measured?

Measuring what matters most - and what can be measured

In attempting to answer this question, there are several useful starting points. Hopkins and Stern (1996), for example, conducted a synthesis of OECD findings from ten countries. They concluded that excellent teachers in all these countries had the following traits in common:

- They made a passionate commitment to doing the best for their students.
- They had a love of children which was enacted in a warm, caring relationship.
- They had strong pedagogical content knowledge.
- They used a variety of models of teaching and learning.

- They had a collaborative working style and regularly worked with other teachers to plan, observe and discuss one another's work.
- They constantly questioned, reflected on, and modified their own practice in light of feedback.

The Education and Training Foundation's Professional Standards (2013) - which articulate what is expected of teachers in the further education sector - define the role of the effective teacher using three broad headings:

1. Professional values and attributes,
2. Professional knowledge and understanding,
3. Professional skills.

The Teachers' Standards - created by the government's Department for Education in 2011 - are intended to inform and support the performance management of teachers working in state schools in England. The standards are gathered under eight umbrella headings. According to the standards, great teachers:

1. Set high expectations which inspire, motivate and challenge pupils,
2. Promote good progress and outcomes by pupils,
3. Demonstrate good subject and curriculum knowledge,
4. Plan and teach well-structured lessons,
5. Adapt teaching to respond to the strengths and needs of all pupils,
6. Make accurate and productive use of assessment,
7. Manage behaviour effectively to ensure a good and safe learning environment, and
8. Fulfil wider professional responsibilities.

There are many such frameworks that seek to set out as succinctly as possible the roles and responsibilities, and the character traits and qualities, shared by the best teachers around the world. But my favoured set of standards is The Danielson Framework (2013) which pithily yet fully sets out what great teachers do. The standards are grouped under the following four headings:

1. Planning and preparation,
2. Classroom,
3. Instruction, and
4. Professional responsibilities.

Under **'planning and preparation'**, Danielson says (and I have taken the liberty to paraphrase and re-word) that teachers should:

Demonstrate a good pedagogical knowledge.
They do this by ensuring that their lesson and unit plans reflect important concepts in the discipline, and accommodate prerequisite relationships among concepts and skills. They ensure they give clear and accurate classroom explanations, give accurate answers to students' questions and feedback to students that furthers learning. And they make interdisciplinary connections in plans and practice.

Maintain a good knowledge of students.
They do this by gathering both formal and informal information about students which they use in planning instruction. They learn students' interests and needs and again use this to inform their planning. They participate in community cultural events.

Write learning outcomes that are of a challenging cognitive level.
They do this by stating student learning not student activity, by ensuring outcomes are central to the discipline and related to those in other disciplines, and by ensuring outcomes can be assessed and differentiated for students of varied ability.

Maintain a knowledge of resources.
They do this using materials from a range of sources including a variety of texts, as well as internet resources and resources from the local community. They participate in professional education courses or professional groups.

Provide coherent instruction.
They do this by ensuring their lessons support instructional outcomes and reflect important concepts, perhaps by creating instructional maps that indicate relationships to prior learning. They provide activities that represent high-level thinking and offer opportunities for student choice. They make use of varied resources and teach structured lessons.

Assess students.
They do this ensuring their lesson plans correspond with assessments and instructional outcomes. They use assessment types that are suitable to the style of outcome and offer a variety of performance opportunities for students. They modify assessments for individual students as needed. They write clear expectations with descriptors for each level of performance. And they design formative assessments which inform minute-to-minute decision making by the teacher during instruction.

Under the '**classroom**' heading, Danielson says that teachers should:

Show respect and rapport for others.
They do this by ensuring they engage in respectful talk, active listening, and turn-taking. They acknowledge students' backgrounds and their lives outside the classroom. Their body language is indicative of warmth and caring shown by teacher and students, and they are polite and encouraging at all times.

Create a culture of learning.
They do this by believing in the value of what is being learned, by setting high expectations for all that are supported through both verbal and non-verbal behaviours, for both learning and participation. They have high expectations of students' work, too, and recognise effort and persistence on the part of students.

Develop effective classroom procedures.
They do this by ensuring the smooth functioning of all routines, with little or no loss of instructional time. They ensure students play an important role in carrying out the routines and that they know what to do and where to move.

Manage student behaviour.
They do this by setting out clear standards of conduct which are regularly referred to during a lesson. There is a notable absence of acrimony between teacher and students concerning behaviour. The teacher is constantly aware of student conduct and takes preventive action when needed. They reinforce positive behaviour.

Make good use of the physical space.
They do this by creating a pleasant, inviting atmosphere, a safe environment that is accessible for all students. They make effective use of physical resources, including technology.

Under **'instruction'**, Danielson says that teachers should:

Communicate effectively.
They do this by having a clarity of lesson purpose, articulating clear directions and procedures specific to the lesson activities. They give clear explanations of concepts and strategies and use correct and imaginative use of language.

Make good use of questioning and classroom discussion.
They do this by asking questions of high cognitive challenge. They use

questions with multiple correct answers or multiple approaches, even when there is a single correct response, and make effective use of student responses and ideas. During discussions, the teacher steps out of the central, mediating role, and focuses on the reasoning exhibited by students, both in give-and-take with the teacher and with their classmates. There are high levels of student participation in discussion.

Engage students in learning.
They do this by promoting enthusiasm, interest, thinking, and problem solving. Learning tasks require high-level student thinking and invite students to explain their thinking. Students are highly motivated to work on all tasks and persistent even when the tasks are challenging. Students are actively working rather than watching while their teacher works. There is a suitable pacing of the lesson: it is neither dragged out nor rushed, and there is time for closure and student reflection.

Use assessment wisely.
They do this by paying close attention to evidence of student understanding, by posing specifically created questions to elicit evidence of student understanding, and by circulating to monitor student learning and to offer feedback. Students assess their own work against established criteria, too.

Be flexible and responsive.
They do this by incorporating students' interests and daily events into a lesson, and by adjusting their instruction in response to evidence of student understanding (or indeed the lack of it).

And under '**professional responsibilities**', Danielson argues that teachers should:

Reflect on their teaching.
They do this by adjusting their practice so that it draws on a repertoire of strategies. They maintain accurate records. They establish routines and systems that track student completion of assignments.

Communicate with families.
They do this by sending appropriate information home regarding the curriculum and student progress. Communication is two-way and there are frequent opportunities for families to engage in the learning process.

Participate in the professional community.
They do this by regularly working with colleagues to share and plan for

student success. They take part in professional courses or communities that emphasise improving practice and engage in school initiatives.

Grow and develop their practice.
They do this by regularly attending courses and workshops and engaging in regular academic reading. They take part in learning networks with colleagues, freely sharing insights.

Show professionalism.
They do this by forging a reputation as being trustworthy. They frequently remind colleagues that students are the highest priority and challenge existing practice in order to put students first.

*

Once you have agreed a set of expectations or standards against which your teachers can be measured for the purposes of performance management, it is important to build a workable system of recording, monitoring and tracking performance against those measures that lead to professional conversations and to the offer of support where performance is deemed to fall short.

I favour a 'balanced scorecard' approach which is a means of aggregating a range of data. That data - soft and hard, narrative and numerical - can be drawn from in-year student progress, end-of-year student outcomes including value added scores, student voice surveys, a teacher's contribution to their own and others' professional development, evidence of professional conduct, a scrutiny of marked student work, evidence of medium- and long-term planning, and so on. The wider the net is cast, the more accurate, fair, and holistic the picture of performance will be.

Of course, such systems are premised on the understanding that no measure of teacher effective is perfect because, as I have said, teaching is a highly complex job. Such systems are also premised on the understanding that data is more than a spreadsheet; it is a conversation. In other words, the data recorded in a scorecard is just that - data. And data is the start of a discussion. Through discussion, data can be converted into meaningful information that will support improvements in teacher effectiveness and, moreover, improvements in outcomes for students.

Whilst accepting its limitations, one advantage of a scorecard is that it can focus attentions where they're needed most and it can help drive positive behaviours.

A scorecard places data centre-stage and puts it in the hands of teachers and school leaders, highlighting good performance to be shared and underperformance to be addressed.

Teachers and school leaders can see their students' progress 'live' and can therefore act on areas of concern in a much more timely fashion and before it is too late to affect change.

The scorecard can also shine a spotlight on those aspects of a teacher's performance that are of particular importance such as target-setting, assessment, and feedback.

Leaders can access - just one-click from login - a 'live' scorecard for their departments. The discussions that flow from the data are crucial because numbers only tell us so much. Professional judgments should always act as the breakwater between data and decision-making, particularly where appraisal outcomes are concerned.

It's also important that a scorecard permeates the whole organisation. Every member of staff working in a school should have a scorecard including the headteacher/principal in order to ensure consistency. No student should be allowed to fall through the net.

A balanced scorecard is only part of the solution, however. The best systems of quality assurance and performance management lead to formative feedback which helps teachers to improve their practice.

In other words, the best performance management processes do not merely draw lines in the sand but provide a roadmap to excellence, and are intrinsically linked to professional development.

In fact, the best systems are not about performance management at all; rather, they are about performance improvement…

If performance improvement feedback is to be effective, it must be based on sound and, more importantly, fair information.

For example, when giving feedback on a lesson observation (which, as I've argued, should still form one piece of the quality assurance jigsaw), the observer should ensure their notes are short, simple observations of things seen, as opposed to subjective remarks about what they would have liked to have seen. Personal opinion, as difficult as it is, should be left at the door of any feedback discussion.

When giving performance feedback, it's also important to remember - common sense, I know, but it's often forgotten in the heat and urgency of the moment - to be polite, professional, and friendly throughout. Even if a teacher's performance is less than we desire, there is nothing to be gained by being confrontational or rude. As such, it's worth contemplating the language we use: our choice of words cannot be in direct conflict with any judgment or outcome. A useful word is 'interesting' because it doesn't imply good or bad - a lesson can be interesting because it is wonderful or because observing it is like rubber-necking a car crash.

Feedback sessions should begin by thanking the teacher for allowing us to observe their lesson, review the evidence of their marked work, or to engage in whatever quality assurance activity has led to the feedback, including taking a look at the data in their scorecard. It's wise to remember that the observed lesson or the scrutinised paperwork was a mere snapshot and not wholly representative of the teacher's overall performance. Our feedback should make this point explicit - just as we would differentiate between a student and their actions when chastising them for misbehaving, we should also differentiate between the teacher as a person and a professional, and the snapshot of their performance we've seen. As well as accepting the limitations of the snapshot, we should remember the Hawthorn Effect, too. By observing something we are changing its very nature.

In the best feedback sessions, the teacher talks a lot more than the leader who is giving the feedback. Not only is this good practice because it encourages the teacher to reflect on their own performance, it also helps the leader to avoid a difficult situation in which they have to impart bad news and invite argument.

Here are some useful questions with which to start a feedback session:
- What went well? What aspects of this performance are you most pleased with?
- If you were to teach this lesson again/mark this work again/etc, what would you do differently and why?
- Can you describe students' starting points and the level of progress they made in this sequence of lessons/with this project?
- Did all students make the progress you hoped they would? How do you know?

Having facilitated a discussion around these questions, we could ask the teacher to summarise their strengths and areas for development as they see them. If the teacher's opinion is less favourable than our own, we'll find ourselves in the enviable position of being able to impart positive, motivational news. If our opinions match, we can feel reassured we're in agreement. If the teacher's opinion is more favourable than our own, we need to find out why by taking an analytical approach, probing into some specifics, for example by asking about individual students and the progress they are making. By drilling down into the detail and analysing small parts of a teacher's performance, we should be able to unmask misunderstandings or misconceptions, and shine a light on those aspects of performance that require improvement.

Hopefully, taking an analytical approach - keeping the discussion professional and focused on the facts not on our own prejudices and preferences - will help the teacher to see that, on reflection, they've been too generous in their initial self-assessment and aspects of their performance can, with time and support, be even better. If not, then firmness may be needed. Being firm and being rude are not synonymous, and neither are being assertive and being aggressive.

Once the feedback has been concluded, we should move the meeting towards action. Whatever the outcome, there is always need of a follow-up. If the teacher's performance is excellent then the action might be to enlist the teacher to share their good practice, to help colleagues improve the quality of their teaching. Perhaps the teacher could lead a CPD session or video a part of their lesson and share it with colleagues in a staff meeting. If the performance has been less than desired then the action might be to engage the teacher in some professional development activities, perhaps observing a colleague and trying out some new approaches in their own classroom.

Whichever path is taken, it is important we end the feedback session with a clear plan of action, complete with reasonable timescales, and an agreed method for the teacher to report back on the progress they are making against this plan.

CHAPTER FOURTEEN
What role can coaching and mentoring play in schools?

In Chapter Fifteen, we will look at teacher professional development in its widest sense. But first let us consider one form of professional development that is gaining traction in schools: coaching and mentoring.

When I wrote the first edition of this book in 2010, coaching was almost unheard of in our schools. It was usual for a trainee teacher and a new teacher in their probation year to be assigned a mentor, a more experienced member of their department who would act as sounding board and confidante. But beyond this, teachers rarely had access to coaching.

Coaching - particularly peer-coaching - is much more common now. However, there is still some misunderstanding about the nature of a coach versus that of a mentor, and the full potential of professional coaching is yet to be realised.

Before we go any further, therefore, let us first define out terms...

A train travels along tracks and cannot deviate from its set route; a coach, by contrast, is able to travel in any direction and go wherever its passengers need it to. Equally, a trainer is someone who follows a set course (hence the term 'training course'); a trainer imparts knowledge in a set order. A coach, however, is someone who can allow him or herself to be led in new and interesting directions, to take detours, in order that the colleague they are coaching is afforded the opportunity to explore the issues that matter most to him or her, and in order to allow that person to find his or her own solution - to arrive at his or her own destination, if you will.

The purpose of coaching is to bring out the best in people by helping them to unlock their potential. Coaching is about teasing out answers from the person being coached through questioning and through challenging their perceptions and understanding. Coaching is about getting the person being coached (the coachee) to explore a situation they've recently experienced (or a situation they are about to experience) from a range of different angles and perspectives so that they might learn from those experiences and so that they might find their own solutions. A coach does not need to know more about a situation than the person being coached; indeed, no expert knowledge is needed and the best coaches are often peers.

What is the difference between coaching and mentoring?

In some contexts, coaching and mentoring are used almost as interchangeable terms. Without doubt they are both valuable processes. It is true that the boundary between them is somewhat permeable and that often the same individuals in schools carry out or participate in both processes. But the CUREE framework distinguishes between three related processes as follows:

• Mentoring is a structured, sustained process for supporting professional students through significant career transitions.

• Specialist coaching is a structured, sustained process for enabling the development of a specific aspect of a professional student's practice.

• Collaborative (Co-) coaching is a structured, sustained process between two or more professional students to enable them to embed new knowledge and skills from specialist sources in day-to-day practice.

Coaching usually takes the form of focused professional dialogue designed to aid the coachee in developing specific skills and to enhance their teaching repertoire. For teachers, coaching often supports experimentation with new classroom strategies. Coaches are not normally in positions of line management in relation to their coachee. Coaching for enhancing teaching and learning is not normally explicitly linked to a career transition. The focus of the coaching is usually selected by the coachee and the process provides opportunities for reflection and problem solving for both coach and coachee.

Mentoring usually takes place at significant career events, such as to support induction or taking on new professional roles. It has an element of 'gatekeeping' and the mentor is almost always someone more senior in the organisation. There is often an organisational motive for the process; for example succession planning. In some cases there is a requirement that the mentor provides documentary evidence of the mentoring process and its outcomes; for example demonstrating that the participant in mentoring has met certain competences.

What is coaching?

Coaching takes many forms: from life coaching to executive coaching – and the aims, purposes and practices can be quite different. So what do all forms of coaching have in common? And what are the general principles of coaching? A study conducted by CUREE in 2005 (which led to the National Framework for Mentoring and Coaching) concluded that:

• The focus of coaching is the in-depth development of specific knowledge, skills and strategies.
• Coaching does not depend on the coach having more experience than the coachee; it can take place between peers and staff at different levels of status and experience.
• Coaching is usually informed by evidence.
• Whilst mentoring can incorporate coaching activity, it tends to focus upon the individual's professional role, often as they move into new roles and take new responsibilities.
• A mentor is usually a more experienced colleague; someone very familiar with a particular culture and role, who has influence and can use their experience to help an individual analyse their situation in order to facilitate professional and career development.

CUREE lists Ten Principles of Coaching in its National Framework:

1. A learning conversation: structured professional dialogue, rooted in evidence from the professional student's practice, which articulates existing beliefs and practices to enable reflection on them.

2. Setting challenging and personal goals: identifying goals that build on what students know and can do already, but could not yet achieve alone, whilst attending to both school and individual priorities.

3. A thoughtful relationship: developing trust, attending respectfully and with sensitivity to the powerful emotions involved in deep professional learning.

4. Understanding why different approaches work: developing understanding of the theory that underpins new practice so it can be interpreted and adapted for different contexts.

5. A learning agreement: establishing confidence about the boundaries of the relationship by agreeing and upholding ground rules that address imbalances in power and accountability.

6. Acknowledging the benefits to the mentors and coaches: recognising and making use of the professional learning that mentors and coaches gain from the opportunity to mentor or coach.

7. Combining support from fellow professional students and specialists: collaborating with colleagues to sustain commitment to learning and relate new approaches to everyday practice; seeking out specialist expertise to extend skills and knowledge and to model good practice.

8. Experimenting and observing: creating a learning environment that supports risk-taking and innovation and encourages professional students to seek out direct evidence from practice.

9. Growing self-direction: an evolving process in which the student takes increasing responsibility for their professional development as skills, knowledge and self-awareness increase.

10. Using resources effectively: making and using time and other resources creatively to protect and sustain learning, action and reflection on a day-to-day basis.

Effective coaching, then, is dependent on the coachee being open and honest with the coach. The coachee needs to be willing to put the plans they make during their coaching session into practice. Accordingly, the National Framework sets out requirements for coachees as well as coaches. Those being coached, the framework says, need to: understand their own learning needs; reflect on their own practice; take an increasingly active role in their own learning; act on what is learned to improve pupil learning.

The National Framework states that coaching is grounded in five key skills:
1. Establishing rapport and trust
2. Listening for meaning
3. Questioning for understanding
4. Prompting action, reflection and learning
5. Developing confidence and celebrating success

Therefore, a coach must: establish high levels of trust; be consistent over time; offer genuine respect; be honest, frank and open; and challenge without threat.

A coach must not: give answers or advice; make judgments; offer counselling; create dependency; impose agendas or initiatives; and confirm long-held prejudice.

What is mentoring?

Mentoring is about leading by example and offering solutions. The mentoring process is focused on developing a person within their professional role - perhaps, for example, helping them to progress within an organisation by stepping a rung up the career ladder. A mentor usually has more experience and knowledge than the mentee - he or she has been there and done that - and the mentor uses his or her own experiences in order to analyse the mentee's situation and offer help and advice on how to deal with it.

The National College of School Leaders defines mentoring in the following terms:

"It's a partnership between a less experienced mentee and the mentor, who uses their extensive professional experience of the mentee's role to help them develop a confident approach to the job. Mentoring is support aimed at professionals in a transition phase in their career, such as moving into the headteacher role.

"Mentors focus on listening and questioning rather than directing the mentee. Their aim is to help the mentee question their practice and come to their own conclusions about steps they may need to take to change or develop their approach to the job.

"It differs from coaching, which is less role-specific and is used for individuals who have been in a post for some time and feel confident in their position and understand the organisation".

Mentoring, like coaching, needs to be structured – quality time must be carved out for the mentoring session to take place and adequate time must also be allocated for preparation and reflection. Mentoring should not be seen as superfluous or somehow peripheral to the real work of a school; it should be integral and planned for. Mentoring sessions should be flexible, allowing for tangential talk, but they should also take place within an agreed, planned framework. Therefore, the mentor needs to plan the mentoring sessions carefully and should evaluate them afterwards.

Effective mentoring takes place when both the mentor and the mentee have thought about the past, present and future: they should analyse what has already happened in order to learn from it, they should consider what is happening right now in order to help shape it, and they should consider what needs to happen in the future in order to plan for it. As mentoring relies on the mentor's prior experience, mentors should be prepared to discuss their experiences, too, and explore what they did when faced with a similar situation, as well as what they learned from it. Unlike a coach, a mentor cannot be passive: they must be active and they must be open and honest.

Furlong and Maynard's 1995 study into the development of a trainee teacher is a useful diversion here because it informs us how new school staff undergo a common process of development: a process which can inform the act of mentoring. The stages are as follows:

Stage 1: Early idealism – student teachers see their role as something that just happens without a great deal of effort on their part...

Stage 2: Personal survival – student teachers are reactive rather than proactive, doing what is necessary to survive...

Stage 3: Dealing with difficulties – student teachers replicate what they believe to be teacherly behaviour...

Stage 4: Hitting a plateau – student teachers begin to gain confidence in their abilities but they act like a teacher rather than think like a teacher...

Stage 5: Moving on – student teachers move on to understand the roles and responsibilities of a teacher.

Although I would define the stages of a trainee teacher's development in slightly different terms, this study is useful because it helps to think in terms of 'common' experiences like this when considering the mentoring process. Why? Because mentoring is likely to follow similar stages of development as the mentee expands his or her experiences, skills and knowledge.

Each mentoring session will be different because they will adapt as the mentee passes through each stage of his/her development. It is likely, too, that the emphasis will pass from the mentor to the mentee as the sessions proceed. The balance of support and challenge will also shift as time moves on. But, broadly speaking, each mentor session will be in three parts:

Past (or 'feedback'):
Setting out and agreeing the objectives for the session; dealing with the issues that have arisen since the last mentoring session, reviewing progress against the targets that were set at the last session or reviewing the mentee's recent experiences.

Present (or 'shaping'):
Discussing situations the mentee is currently involved in and situations which are enfolding presently; debating how he or she has dealt with the situation so far and how he or she intends to deal with the situation next, what he or she intends to do next.

Future (or 'planning'):
Learning from past and present experiences and allowing them to redefine the mentee in terms of their knowledge, skills and experience; stepping back and reflecting on how the mentee has developed and grown, and discussing how he or she will apply this learning to future situations; predicting and planning for future events.

What are the benefits of coaching and mentoring in schools?

The benefits of coaching and mentoring for the individuals being supported are perhaps obvious: they will become more motivated and their confidence will grow; their knowledge and skills will be enhanced and their experience will be enlarged – because they will learn more about themselves and more about their jobs as a result of the process.

But coaching and mentoring also benefit the organisation: staff who are motivated and confident in their work will show greater degrees of loyalty towards their school. This, in turn, will improve levels of recruitment and retention and aid the development of sustainable leadership – in other words, schools can grow their own leaders. But coaching and mentoring can also foster effective and genuine sharing between colleagues, as well as between departments and faculties. Sharing best practice helps to reduce inconsistencies and helps improve performance across the school.

Coaching and mentoring can be used to help school staff deal with a variety of situations including:
- managing student behaviour
- increasing student performance
- developing and fostering team spirit and effective team working
- developing staff who are new to their roles and responsibilities
- helping staff with career development

- improving teachers' performance and avoiding capability proceedings or disciplinaries
- developing lesson planning practices and improving teaching and learning
- developing marking and assessment practices
- supporting colleagues on teacher training programmes, as well as NQTs

However, coaching and mentoring will only be effective in these situations if the school invests in them and takes them seriously. Coaching and mentoring need to be a part of a school's everyday working practices. There need to be appropriate structures and systems in place which encourage coaching and mentoring and which ensure it is a long-term solution. If this is so, coaching and mentoring will reap longer-term benefits.

In practice, this means investing time and money into coaching and mentoring and creating links with other organisations and networks. For example, coaching and mentoring should be linked to performance management. Coaching and mentoring should also be linked to the school improvement plan: developing coaching and mentoring can be an objective in its own right and the act of coaching and mentoring can be listed as a resource to bring about the completion of other objectives in the plan.

Coaching and mentoring should also be a part of the school's planned programme of professional development, perhaps even a whole-school INSET event because staff may need training before being coached/mentored or indeed before becoming a coach or mentor. This training may be around the notion of 'contracting': of agreeing the terms of the coaching/mentoring sessions and agreeing the intended outcomes; or it may be around the skills needed to question and challenge, to persevere and press for firm commitments.

Coaching and performance management might be linked in the following ways: Coaching might be used by managers to address concerns raised through performance management. Evidence emerging from coaching might be used to inform the coachee's own performance management. Participants might elect to use coaching as a means of addressing an area of development identified through performance management.

The future of coaching and mentoring in schools

As I said at the beginning of this chapter, coaching and mentoring are becoming ever more integral to the way schools operate - not least thanks to the introduction of 'teaching schools'. Schools - not universities or colleges – are becoming the places for training new teachers: more and more students are applying for graduate teaching posts rather than PGCE courses, and more and more schools are taking on the responsibility for training their own teachers rather than accommodating ITT students from other providers.

The concept of 'teaching schools' was introduced in 2011 in the coalition government's 'Importance of Teaching' white paper and is based on the existing model of teaching hospitals. The basic principle is that teaching schools will build on existing school-based initial teaching training programmes and existing continuing professional development programmes. The difference is that teaching schools will also:

• Train new entrants to the profession by working with other partners such as universities
• Lead peer-learning and professional development programmes, including the designation and deployment of specialist leaders of education (SLEs)
• Identify and nurture leadership potential
• Lead a local network of schools and other partners in order to improve the quality of teaching and learning
• Help form a national network of schools to support them with innovation and the transfer of knowledge
• Be at the heart of a new school improvement strategy or system that puts responsibility on the profession and on schools rather than on local authorities or the government

In his paper on the subject of teaching schools, David Hargreaves argues that, "It will not be enough for teaching schools to continue [with the traditional model] of professional development. Their challenging task is to raise professional development to a new level through the exemplary use and dissemination of joint practice development [which] "captures a process that is truly collaborative, not one-way; the practice is being improved, not just moved from one person or place to another":

Joint practice development gives birth to innovation and grounds it in the routines of what teachers naturally do. Innovation is fused with and grows out of practice, and when the new practice is demonstrably superior, escape from the poorer practice is expedited.

If joint practice development replaced sharing good practice in the professional vocabulary of teachers, we would, I believe, see much more effective practice transfer in the spirit of innovation that is at the heart of a self-improving system.

"Mentoring and coaching between schools," Hargreaves argues, "are at the heart of this effective practice transfer. A school that has not developed a strong mentoring and coaching culture is not likely to be successful either at moving professional knowledge and skills to partners or at rising to the level of joint practice development." He says effective use of coaching and mentoring is a means of nurturing talent and is of particular importance in leadership development "since leaders learn best with and from outstanding leaders."

He argues that effective mentoring and coaching in schools is defined as follows: "The school contributes to external courses on mentoring and coaching within professional development and has experience of the use of external mentors and coaches (e.g. from business and industry) for both staff and students. The school is piloting new approaches to mentoring and coaching, such as a system of online student-to-student mentoring and coaching between schools".

It is clear, therefore, that coaching and mentoring is vital if schools are serious about developing sustainable leadership (in other words, they wish to 'grow their own leaders') and if schools wish to engage in genuine continuing professional development; but coaching and mentoring is also becoming increasingly important as schools become autonomous of local authority control and move towards the new model of 'teaching schools'. It is vital, too, if they wish to become members of a network of 'family' of schools responsible for developing their own staff and for leading their own programmes of school improvement.

Professional learning communities

As well as coaching and mentoring, professional learning communities are a way of engaging colleagues in the process of sharing best practice and developing their professional practice...

In 'Drive', Daniel Pink explores what motivates people at work. He argues that people tend to be motivated by autonomy – in other words, being accorded control over the way they work; mastery – being good at their jobs and getting better; and purpose – doing a job which is considered meaningful and worthy.

One way to promote autonomy, mastery, and purpose is through the establishment of professional learning communities in which teachers are provided with the time, space and – perhaps most importantly of all – the safety net they need in order to feel able and supported to take risks, to try out new teaching methods without fear or favour.

Joyce and Showers' report, 'Student achievement through staff development' (2002), explores the idea of professional learning communities further.

The authors argue that teaching has at least three times the effect on student achievement as any other factor and assert that teaching is best improved through experimentation. In other words, teachers need to be accorded the opportunity to try out new teaching strategies and then to candidly discuss with colleagues what worked and what did not.

Joyce and Showers suggest the following method:

Identify training needs:
Here, teachers ask themselves 'What do we feel are our most pressing needs? And 'What do our results tell us? Then a list of 10-20 ideas for improvement is drawn up, combined, compromised and prioritised into one common goal. This common goal is focused on a process designed to produce better outcomes which will directly affect students' experiences.

Training is devised:
At this stage, training is planned in the following sequence…
- Knowledge – new theories and rationale are explained
- Demonstration – new theories are modelled
- Practice – teachers try out the theories for themselves
- Peer coaching – teachers work together to solve the problems and answer the questions which arise during the 'practice' stage.

Training is delivered:
Now, the above training takes place over a period of time and is continually evaluated.

Joyce and Showers found that teachers must practice new methods 20-25 times if they are to learn how to use them as effectively as they do their usual methods.

There is a lot of research which underlines the importance of deliberate practice in achieving mastery and all insist that practice must be carried out over a long period of time. Most notably there is the '10,000-hour rule' propounded by Malcolm Gladwell in Outliers and Matthew Syed in Bounce. The argument here is that in order to become an expert you must accrue at least 10,000 hours of practice. Anders Ericsson, from whose seminal study of violinists in Berlin the 10,000 hour rule purportedly arises, has said he never insisted on this figure as a hard and fast rule - the number of hours of practice required to achieve mastery, he says, depends upon the individual's starting point, the skill being practiced and the nature of the practice. However, Ericsson does still insist that it is only the amount of practice that distinguishes the novice from the expert.

As well as dedicating a significant amount of time to practising a new teaching strategy, Joyce and Showers also warn that the first few attempts at trying out a new classroom technique might fail but that the teacher must remain positive and keep trying. This process of experimentation works best – according to Joyce and Showers – when teachers:

- Practice the use of the new methods repeatedly over a period of time
- Monitor the effect of the new methods on students
- Ask students their opinions on the new methods, garnering further suggestions
- Bring issues to peer coaching sessions for discussion
- Help and support others with their experimentation

It is important that leaders support experimentation by modelling what Joyce and Showers call an 'improvement and renewal' style of leadership. That is to say, they display an emphatic belief that it is always possible to get better, no matter how good you already are. And they display the belief that the factors which most affect student outcomes are in students' and teachers' control. They do not blame achievement on socio-economic factors nor suggest that ability is innate. They do not accept low standards.

Leaders can also promote improvement by:
- Promoting collaboration
- Ensuring improvement meetings are frequent and well-attended
- Expecting a high standard of peer coaching
- Expecting experimentation to be supported by evidence
- Being positive and promoting the importance of teachers

Geoff Petty, an education writer, has shared a useful model for improving teaching. It goes like this:
1. Explore the context: understand the key issues in ensuring success for all
2. Explore present practice: understand how we teach at present
3. Explore the pedagogy: understand what other teaching strategies could

improve teaching
4. Plan experimentation and implementation: decide ways to teach better
5. Improve and coach-in strategies: develop strategies whilst receiving support from a peer coach
6. Monitor: monitor experimentation to ensure they make a difference to students
7. Share and celebrate success: report on experiments and share strategies
8. Embed practice: new strategies are agreed and put into planning for the whole team to implement

What professional learning communities do best is encourage risk-taking. Because they are about developing teaching expertise rather than judging colleagues' abilities, they encourage colleagues to try out new ways of teaching, some which will work and some of which will not. Risk-taking and innovation are key to the long-term development of teaching because they help us as professionals to keep on getting better over time.

As lead learners, teachers should model the process of learning for their students. We need to show our students that we are also learning all the time and that we are unafraid of trying new things even if that means we sometimes make mistakes. Actually, not "even if that means we make mistakes" but "exactly because it means we make mistakes"… After all, to make mistakes is to learn; to learn is to increase our IQs. As Samuel Beckett wrote back in 1884, "Ever tried? Ever failed? Try again. Fail again. Fail better." Teachers need to model the "growth mindset" approach pioneered by Carol Dweck.

Professional learning communities also encourage teachers to do exactly what we want all of our students to do in order to achieve success: namely, to work outside their comfort zones, to try something difficult. And setting ourselves tough tasks is also to be encouraged because challenge leads to deeper learning and greater achievement. Challenge is, after all, a central feature of outstanding learning. If you think back to a time when you've felt challenged either personally or professionally, you'll probably recall feeling discomfort. But, once you'd overcome the challenge and achieved, the sense of success with which you were rewarded felt far greater than if you'd achieved something easy without even breaking into a sweat.

Dylan Wiliam - of the Institute of Education, King's College London - suggests a six-part structure for professional learning community workshops. He advocates following the same structure each time so that all colleagues come to know what is expected. This structure is as follows:

1. Introduction.
Approximately five minutes to share learning intentions for the workshop.

2. Starter.
Approximately five minutes as a warm-up or to share some recent positive and negative experiences.

3. Feedback.
Between twenty-five and fifty minutes for colleagues to talk about what they've done since the last workshop, perhaps by talking through their professional development plan. It is important that all colleagues prepare for this session and are clear and detailed in the experiences they talk about including outlining what went well and what did not, and what they have learned from the experience.

4. New learning.
Between twenty and forty minutes to discuss new learning, learning which can then be put into practice between this workshop and the next one. This might involve watching a video, discussing a book, and so on.

5. Professional development planning.
Approximately fifteen minutes to update professional development plans and organise with colleagues future peer observations and work scrutinies.

6. Review of learning.
Approximately five minutes to recap on the core learning from this workshop.

Each workshop, Wiliam says, should last between seventy-five minutes and two hours.

Garmston and Wellman share 7 Ps of effective collaboration which may be useful in setting a supportive tone at these professional learning community workshops:

1. Pausing
This is about allowing all participants time to think, reflect on what's been said and develop their understanding.

2. Paraphrasing
This is about the workshop leader reiterating key points, repeating back what others say in order that all participants can hear and understand what is being said.

3. Probing
This is about the workshop leader asking questions and requesting participants develop their ideas further.

4. Putting ideas on the table
This is about welcoming everybody's input and greeting ideas with respect; it is also about the workshop leader accepting that there are different points of view which need to be considered and thought-through without prejudice.

5. Paying attention to self and others
This is about thinking through how to say something in a way that does not offend others nor incite argument.

6. Presuming positive intentions
This is about presuming others mean well and trying to prevent argument.

7. Pursuing balance between advocacy and inquiry
This is about striking the right balance between inquiring into others' ideas before advocating your own.

Dylan Wiliam says that the most effective learning communities run for two years, meet monthly to discuss new ideas and to share experiences, and identify dedicated time between meetings for colleagues to carry out peer observations and to plan collaboratively. Professor Coe at the University of Durham agrees that the best professional development is sustained over the long-term, content-focused, active and evidence-based.

Dylan Wiliam advocates starting with the content then moving on to the process. Content is about choosing the appropriate evidence, formulating the initial ideas; process is about according people with choice and flexibility, encouraging them to take small steps forward with support but also with accountability. In other words, content is about the what? and process is about the how?

Another way of looking at it is this…

As a collective, we should decide on the strategy – what aspect of pedagogy we need to focus on first; and then individual teachers should decide on the techniques – how they intend to embed this strategy, what practical changes they plan to make. For example, a school may decide that its first collective focus should be on improving the quality of the formative feedback given to students by teachers and by students themselves. Then individual teachers are given the autonomy to trial new methods of giving and acting on feedback in their classes. In other words, individual teachers take ownership of their own professional development. After all, teaching is all about personality. Every teacher has a different personality and therefore a different way of teaching. Such differences should be embraced not eradicated. We want human beings at the helm of our children's learning not automatons, after all.

CHAPTER FIFTEEN
What does effective professional development look like in schools?

In Chapter Thirteen I argued in favour of a new approach to quality assurance, moving from a system of performance management to one of performance improvement. Rather than relying on high-stakes, graded lesson observations, I said, we should adopt a 'balanced scorecard' approach whereby we aggregate a broad range of data in order to paint a more accurate, fair and holistic picture of a teacher's performance. I also argued that quality assurance data should lead to performance feedback aimed at helping teachers to improve. Quality assurance systems, in other words, should not merely draw a line in the sand but provide a roadmap to excellence.

In Chapter Fourteen I talked about the importance of coaching and mentoring, and of the role professional learning communities can play in helping teachers to act on feedback and improve their practice. Coaching and other forms of professional development are, after all, the natural next step in this process: once feedback has been shared, we need to provide teachers with opportunities to engage in quality professional development activities which will help them to improve aspects of their performance.

In this chapter, I'd like to explore professional development in a wider sense and focus on what effective professional development looks like in practice...

Let us start with this important - yet oft forgotten - truth about education: teachers - and what happens in their classrooms - are the only real drivers of positive change in our schools. The only way to improve the quality of teaching, therefore, is to improve the quality of our teachers. And the only way to improve the quality of our teachers is to treat them fairly and with respect, and to train them well and continue to develop them throughout their careers.

Improving the quality of teachers requires systems of collaboration so that professional development becomes an everyday, collaborative exercise not an end of year 'sheep-dip' activity 'done to' teachers by school leaders.

Improving the quality of teachers requires professional development to be personalised, tailored to meet individual needs, so that it is made meaningful and encompasses all aspects of self-improvement activity - such as reading research, watching colleagues teach, working with a coach, and engaging in lesson study - not just attending a generic, formal training course.

Improving the quality of teachers also requires professional development to recognise hard work in all its forms - even the quiet, 'just doing my job' kind - and to encourage rather than stifle team-work, and to favour collaboration over competition.

In short, improving the quality of teachers - as I argued earlier - is about fairness and professionalism; it's about building a mature, adult culture in which teachers and school leaders work together in the best interests of their students to improve the quality of teaching in their schools and to do so without fear or favour.

So how can schools ensure that they provide high quality professional development for their staff and do so without drilling a big hole in their diminishing budgets?

The Standard for Teacher Professional Development (2016) - together with the ETF Professional Standards and the DfE Teachers' Standards - may just hold the key. The five strands of the Standard are as follows:

1. Professional development should have a focus on improving and evaluating student outcomes.
2. Professional development should be underpinned by robust evidence and expertise.
3. Professional development should include collaboration and expert challenge.
4. Professional development programmes should be sustained over time.
5. Professional development must be prioritised by senior leadership.

So what does this look like in practice and how can schools deliver it?

As the Standard suggests, the most effective professional development is collaborative and driven by teachers. Professional development, therefore, should involve responding to advice and feedback from colleagues, and reflecting systematically on the effectiveness of lessons and approaches to teaching. This might take the form of peer-observations and feedback, of peer-coaching, or of more formal lesson study activities. It might also take the form of peer-to-peer work scrutiny, both of students' marked work and assessment records, and of medium- and long-term planning documentation.

Whatever form it takes, the best professional development gives ownership to staff and creates the time and space needed for them to work together, sharing best practice and learning from each other's mistakes.

Another way to ensure that professional development is effective is to make it an unmissable event, tailored to meet the differing needs of departments and teachers. Every member of staff should recognise the importance of professional development as a mandatory part of their jobs – not as a voluntary extra. But they'll only do that when professional development is worth engaging in and it will only be worth engaging in when it is relevant, timely, keenly focused on real classroom practice, and genuinely and tangibly impactful.

In order to ensure relevance and focus, professional development should be influenced by research evidence but informed by context. In other words, it should take its lead from what research indicates works best (for example, John Hattie's meta-analyses as articulated in his book Visible Learning or the Sutton Trust's useful toolkit) but be mindful of the unique circumstances of each school, subject, teacher and cohort of students.

As well as being unmissable, professional development should be regular, embedded and joined-up. Professional development should be seen as a collaborative enterprise involving all staff working together, rather than something which is 'done to' them by senior leaders.

Professional development also works best when it performs the twin functions of innovation and mastery. In other words, professional development should not just be about learning new ways of working – professional development for innovation - although this is undoubtedly important. Rather, it should also be about helping teachers to get better at something they already do – professional development for mastery. Professional development for mastery is about recognising what already works well and what should therefore be embedded, consolidated, built upon, and shared.

Postscript to Chapter Fifteen

In this chapter I have argued in favour of professional development as a means of improving the quality of teachers and, therefore, the quality of teaching in our schools. However, in recent years - and certainly since I wrote the first edition of this book - school budgets have been cut to the bone and professional development has often been an early casualty.

It is certainly true that school leaders are facing the biggest challenge of their professional lives: they're simultaneously trying to balance the books amid a national funding crisis and provide the resources required to bolster teaching and learning and improve outcomes for learners.

According to National Audit Office data from 2017, schools face an 8 per cent real-terms cut worth £3 billion by 2020. More than half of schools already lack enough income to cover their expenditure. In 2015/16, for example, 53% of multi-academy trusts spent more than their income compared with just 25% the previous year. Governors in some schools have threatened - for the very first time - to go on strike rather than agree underfunded budgets. In West Sussex, for example, governors have written to their local MPs warning that they will refuse to sign off budgets or carry out supervisory work. Some head teachers are considering cutting school hours by, for example, running a four-day week whereby children work at home on the fifth day in order to save on heating, lighting, cleaning and transport costs. And an increasing number of schools have begun asking parents for cash to help plug their funding gaps. According to a recent survey by PTA UK (a charity which represents a network of parent associations in schools), for example, more than a third of parents say they have been asked to donate money to their child's school because of an inadequacy of school funding.

As such, headteachers/principals are having to decide which subjects to stop teaching, which teachers to make redundant, which classes to merge, and which services - careers advice, the school library, mental health counselling - to cut or curtail. At times like these, the first axe to fall is often the sword of Damocles that's been hovering above the staff development budget because - when faced with tough choices - training budgets start to look like a luxury.

Research by the Teacher Development Trust in 2017 suggests that as many as 20,000 teachers in England were without a training budget. Professional development budgets were already small in comparison with high-performing nations like Finland. Secondary schools in England spend an average of just 0.37% of their budgets on staff training; primary schools, meanwhile, spend just 0.65%. But now, faced with big budget cuts, some schools are struggling to sustain even these low levels of spending. The TDT study found that 600 of the schools surveyed had already wiped out their professional development budgets.

But does it have to be this way..? Professional development, as I have argued throughout this chapter, matters.

In reporting its findings, the TDT warned that investment in professional training should remain a priority and that students deserved to be taught by teachers with up-to-date skills.

The Department for Education, responding to the study, said: "Continued professional development is vital for all teachers to help improve their knowledge and skills. We trust heads to make the right decisions for their staff and… to invest in high quality training and development."

In an address to the College of Teaching in February 2017, Education Secretary Justine Greening said: "One of the things I learned early on in my career as an accountant was the importance of being part of a profession – a community of experts with a shared commitment to best practice. [As such] I want professional development to run like a golden thread throughout teachers' careers, with high-quality, evidence-based development available for all teachers. Teachers are the experts on teaching, and so I want the profession to lead on improving schools."

And the Education Select Committee, in a report published in February 2017, recommended that the government roll out an annual entitlement of professional development for all teachers in order to boost retention rates. The committee strongly recommended subject-specific professional development in order to ensure the "maintenance and acquisition of subject knowledge" among teachers.

What's more, professional development is at the heart of the Teachers' Standards which state that all teachers should: keep their knowledge and skills up-to-date and be self-critical; take responsibility for improving teaching through appropriate professional development, responding to advice and feedback from colleagues; demonstrate knowledge and understanding of how students learn and how this has an impact on teaching; have a secure knowledge of relevant subjects and curriculum areas; reflect systematically on the effectiveness of lessons and approaches to teaching; and know and understand how to assess relevant subjects and curriculum areas.

In short, cutting back on professional development - even at a time of unprecedented austerity - should be regarded as counterproductive, short-sighted and evidence-averse.

*

Robert Sternberg, the American psychologist, argues that "The major factor in whether people achieve expertise is not some fixed prior ability, but purposeful engagement." The Professor of Psychology at Stanford University, Carol Dweck, meanwhile, believes that "Your basic qualities are things you can cultivate through your efforts. Although people may differ in every which way...everyone can change and grow through application and experience." And the author Dan Heath asserts that "To practice isn't to declare, I'm bad. To practice is to declare, I can be even better." To which sentiment we might add Doug Lemov's statement that "With practice you'll get stronger results if you spend your time practising the most important things."

Professional development provides teachers with opportunities to practice and, through practice, to improve.

Teaching is not a job; it is a profession. As such, teachers and school leaders should take seriously the continuous development of their knowledge and skills. After all, we wouldn't want to be operated on by an unqualified, unskilled surgeon with out of date knowledge. We wouldn't want to fly in a plane piloted by an amateur. So why would we want our students to be educated by unqualified, unskilled teachers and our schools to be run by unqualified, unskilled leaders?

International comparisons teach us that the most successful education systems in the world – such as the oft-cited Finland which I lucky enough to visit a couple of years ago – recruit the best teachers, train them well, and continue to value and develop them throughout their careers.

Judith Little, an American educational researcher who works at the University of California, Berkeley, says that most successful schools have four things in common and these shared traits can be key to the kind of quality, staff-driven professional development I have been advocating in this book.

1. Teachers talk about learning.
Professional development activities are dedicated to talking about lessons, about students, and about teaching and learning in general. CPD opportunities are rarely used to discuss administrative matters, this is done by other means such as email, memos, a chat in the corridor, and so on.

2. Teachers observe each other.
Professional development provides opportunities for teachers to engage in a planned programme of peer learning reviews and feedback. Peer learning reviews are then followed by constructive, focused professional conversations about how teachers can improve and about how teachers can share good practice and celebrate each other's skills and talents. Peer learning reviews and unseen observations, along with learning walks, allow teachers to take genuine snapshots of what happens every day, snapshots which can provide helpful suggestions for improvement as well as recognise and then reward genuine success.

3. Teachers plan together.
Judith Little talks of teachers writing lesson plans together, teaching the same lessons, then discussing them. I do not believe that it is necessary to have individual lesson plans because detailed session-by-session plans can encourage rigidity and 'teaching to the plan', not the kind of teaching which responds pragmatically to students' needs.

So Little's 'teachers plan together' could be interpreted as teachers talking to each other about their medium- and long-term planning, and about their marking and students' work. Professional development could involve teachers routinely scrutinising each other's work and moderating each other's assessments, perhaps engaging in a process of peer review of each other's mark-books and students' work.

4. Teachers teach each other.
Professional development events and meetings are transformed into professional learning communities (such as those I described in Chapter Fourteen) which provide opportunities for teachers to share practice and comment on what they've tried and what worked and what didn't. These sessions are staff-led, collaborative enterprises not opportunities for leaders and managers to stand and deliver.

*

If we agree that professional development is important and should be invested in, then what should be the focus of teachers' development activities? What teaching approaches or strategies are proven to lead to the largest academic gains for students?

First of all, the best professional development is sustained. In other words, it focuses on one thing at a time and does so over a long period. Why? Because being an expert teacher – like being an expert at anything – takes a lot of hard work and effort. However, when a teacher practises their trade they must do so for a long period of time and must do so deliberately because, as Doug Lemov says in his book Practice Perfect, practice does not make perfect, it makes permanent. In other words, if teachers practice the wrong things or the wrong techniques then they will simply embed these bad habits into their everyday practice; they will not get better.

Deliberate practice is a focused and collaborative exercise. Deliberate practice is what top athletes do. Top athletes are coached in one area of their performance at a time – say, their back-hand, their swing, their positioning on the starting blocks – and are given immediate feedback by their coach, before reflecting on that advice and making small corrective adjustments.

This is a process not dissimilar to what teachers do as trainees and newly qualified teachers. They constantly receive feedback and reflect on their own performance before making tweaks. Their mentor acts as a critical friend.

Teachers should continue in this vein throughout their teaching careers not become isolated or start developing bad habits. Of course, this is not easy because engaging in deliberate practice, to continually reflect on their performance, is to expose themselves to their own failures, to pick apart their mistakes. Deliberate practice is also time-consuming and takes real effort and resilience.

Doug Lemov suggests that effective professional development should be about the following three things:

1. *Practising the 20%*
Lemov argues that teachers should apply 'the law of the vital few' because, with practice, they'll get better results if they dedicate most of their professional development time to practising the 20% of things which create 80% of the value (or, in a different interpretation, the 20% of things which have the same value as the other 80% combined). In other words, teachers need to prioritise their professional development content.

2. Designing the drills

Through focusing on fewer things at any one time, it is possible to work on those things with a greater level of intensity. Designing the drills is about thinking through the ways in which teachers can best practise the 20%; it is about designing methods which will have the biggest impact on everyday performance. In other words, teachers need to find the best form for their professional development to take.

3. Shortening the feedback loop

Once teachers have chosen their 20% and decided on the methods by which they're going to improve them, they need to find ways of getting regular feedback on their improving performance because one of the most effective ways of improving their teaching practice is to improve the quality and immediacy of the feedback they get.

Teachers therefore need to ensure that professional development provides opportunities to get feedback on their teaching which can help them 'tweak' what they do and can be put into immediate use. In other words, they need to routinely evaluate their performance and evaluate the effectiveness of the professional development in which they engage.

CHAPTER SIXTEEN
How can school leaders manage the business?

As I explained in Chapter One, school leaders are effectively the directors of medium-sized businesses and, as such, they carry a director's responsibility for ensuring that their business is managed according to the law. This is never more important than when managing the school's finances, the school site and the school's digital infrastructure.

It is likely that your school has a finance manager and/or support from your local authority but, nevertheless, the senior team should have a good understanding of the school's budget and should be involved in agreeing its spending priorities - this not only fosters collective responsibility and accountability but also encourages sustainable leadership. Senior leaders should understand how the school's budget is divided and how fiscal decisions are reached.

It is also likely that your school has a site manager or that the responsibility for managing your site is contracted out; but senior leaders should again understand their role in ensuring the school is compliant with health and safety legislation and that the site is kept safe. They should also understand their role with regards to safeguarding – as should every member of staff.

Your school will probably have a network manager and may have an ICT development manager but the senior team should still understand how ICT is used and what the school's priorities are for future ICT developments; the senior team should also be involved in setting direction when it comes to further investments in the school's digital infrastructure.

Let's look at each of these aspects of managing the business in turn:

*

Finance

Good financial management can, I believe, be summed up in 3 Ps: prudence, planning, and prioritisation:

Prudence
It is important that school leaders are prudent; it is important that they carefully consider every expense and that they ensure they are achieving value for money. School leaders are accountable for their fiscal decisions and should be confident that any spending they sanction is necessary and represents the best value they can find. Schools need effective processes and procedures in place for contracting, tendering and purchasing. Schools should also have systems in place for producing regular monitoring reports which show the school's current financial position, its future position (budget forecast) and any potential risks.

Planning
School leaders should have a financial plan and this should be linked to the school improvement plan. All the actions on the school improvement plan should, in turn, be costed. Although some costs will be unforeseen, the majority of spending should be planned for. By planning ahead, schools can ensure that their spending will have a long-term impact. Looking ahead and predicting the future is a vital skill for senior leaders. Schools should also have an asset management plan to keep track of their valuable resources and to ensure that those assets are kept serviced and safe.

Prioritisation
When planning the budget, it is important that school leaders prioritise their spending according to the impact the spending will have on students' learning. It is also important that spending is prioritised according to what will have the biggest impact and what will improve most young people's lives.

Balancing the books...

School leaders need to understand where their school's money comes from and how it should be spent. School funding formulas are ever changing and there is little to be gained by setting out here how schools are funded - indeed, I did so in the first edition but that information was soon outdated. So I will not linger on the minutiae of income and expenditure, except to say this...

Income

The largest proportion of income is likely to be based on per pupil funding - that is to say, the amount of money the government pays you to educate each child admitted onto your roll. There will be additional funding for aspects such as premises, special needs, local and national initiatives, and so on. The bulk of post-16 funding is also based on student numbers. Other sources of significant income include: the pupil premium; literacy and numeracy catch-up funding; and lettings.

Expenditure

The single largest expenditure for schools is, by some distance, staffing. Teaching staff are the most costly but do not underestimate the cost of support staff, and clerical and admin staff.

Separate but related to staffing is the cost of expenses such as training courses, staff travel and supply teachers. When planning for additional staffing, it is important to include the full costs, including actual salary, as well as national insurance and pension contributions.

Other major sources of expenditure include: premises costs such as electricity, gas and water; learning resources such as books, paper, IT hardware and software; supplies and services such as photocopying, catering contractors; the costs of repairs, and health and safety maintenance and inspections such as legionella and PAT testing; and other site costs such as insurance, running a school minibus, and so on.

*

The school site

The most important aspects of managing the school site are: health and safety, and safeguarding and child protection.

Health and Safety

In managing health and safety, it is important to ensure that appropriate risk assessments are conducted and implemented, and that systems are in place for identifying and responding to health and safety issues. It is also important that there is a system for ensuring that all accidents are recorded and that action is taken to address issues of concern and to minimise risks. Most health and safety matters can be more easily managed and kept track of if line management responsibilities are clear and all job descriptions include appropriate responsibility for managing health and safety issues. It is also vital that there is a programme of external support and that training is used as appropriate.

Health and safety law - and the requirements of local authorities for the reporting of health and safety concerns - often changes but what remains largely consistent is that the job of managing health and safety is concerned with:

- Coordinating the completion and revision of risk assessments and ensuring they are understood and adhered to
- Conducting site checks (usually with a link governor and a contractor or local authority advisor) to ensure the site is safe and to identify areas for improvement such as signage, building repairs and security in order to minimise risks
- Developing effective systems for identifying and responding to health and safety issues
- Managing the system by which accidents are reported and followed up on
- Ensuring fire drills take place termly and a fire log is kept which details each drill and accounts for every fire alarm, fire extinguisher, sprinkler and smoke alarm and records how often they have all been tested
- Developing clear accountability, for example by including line management responsibilities in job descriptions
- Coordinating a programme of support and training for staff
- Providing appropriate first aid provision – both in terms of administering and administrating: in other words, making sure there is appropriate first aid cover, appropriate first aid equipment, and that all instances of first aid are recorded and followed up on
- Ensuring there are effective procedures in place for a speedy and safe evacuation or invacuation of the site in the event of a fire, a loss of power, inclement weather or a bomb threat
- Ensuring there is an effective system in place for maintaining the school's physical assets. This means coordinating a cycle of maintenance, overseeing the testing of equipment (such as PAT testing electrical equipment or testing PE equipment, as well as COSSH testing and testing for legionella)
- Managing the school's programme of educational visits, ensuring health and safety and safeguarding checks have been completed, that students' medical needs have been taken care of and that risk assessments have been completed

Safeguarding

Safeguarding has assumed priority status in schools in recent years, not least because of the prominence given to it by Ofsted. In her commentary to Ofsted's 2009/10 Annual Report, Her Majesty's Chief Inspector wrote: "Safeguarding...is an issue addressed not only with increasing sureness by those responsible for keeping children and learners safe, but one felt keenly by those most vulnerable to harm and neglect."

Since that time, we have seen two changes of Chief Inspector and yet safeguarding has remained a focus. Of course, it is only right that safeguarding should be viewed as important because there can be no issue of greater concern to parents and carers, or indeed to schools, than the safety of their children.

Although the Ofsted framework has changed a couple of times since 2010, and the number of judgment areas has been slashed, safeguarding has continued to feature strongly in the 2012 and the 2015 inspection schedule – not least in the judgment of personal development, behaviour and welfare, and in overall effectiveness. Safeguarding also runs through the leadership and management judgment like the letters in a stick of rock. A new inspection framework is due in 2019 and so far there is little to suggest that the focus on - and the way of judging - safeguarding will change in any significant way.

So what is safeguarding? The definition used in the Children Act 2004 and in the Department for Education guidance document 'Working together to safeguard children', (which focuses on safeguarding and promoting children's and learners' welfare), can be summarised as follows:

- Protecting children and learners from maltreatment
- Preventing impairment of children's and learners' health or development
- Ensuring that children and learners are growing up in circumstances consistent with the provision of safe and effective care
- Undertaking that role so as to enable those children and learners to have optimum life chances and to enter adulthood successfully.

The governing bodies of maintained schools and local authorities must comply with the Education Act 2002. The Department for Education guidance document, 'Safeguarding children and safer recruitment in education', makes it clear that schools must provide a safe environment and take action to identify and protect any children or young people who are at risk of significant harm.

In particular, schools are required:

- To prevent unsuitable people from working with children and young people;
- To promote safe practice and challenge unsafe practice;
- To ensure that staff receive the necessary training for their roles; and
- To work in partnership with other agencies providing services for children and young people.

Local authorities, meanwhile, have a duty:
- To provide model policies and procedures on all aspects of safeguarding;
- To ensure that schools are aware of, and comply with, their responsibilities.

Ofsted produced a 'good practice' report in September 2011 which identified the features of exceptionally good safeguarding and its findings - which remain valid - are worth considering here.

Ofsted say that there is no reason why good practice in safeguarding should not be a feature of every school; the practice described in its report is replicable in every school. Its features of best practice not only comply with the legal requirements but often move beyond them. Safeguarding, as detailed in their report, is not seen as a burden but as a "reasonable and essential part of the fabric of the school".

The report pays attention to the "meticulous and systematic implementation of policies and routines" but shows how it should also involve every member of the school community. 19% of the schools who contributed to the report were judged to be outstanding in their safeguarding procedures in 2009/10.

The key word when it comes to safeguarding for both inspectors and schools is 'reasonable' and it is around the interpretation of 'reasonable' that a mythology has emerged. In the report, Ofsted attempts to set the record straight: "Ofsted does not require schools to build walls around play areas; it does not expect schools to seek CRB [now called DBS] checks on casual visitors to schools, including parents; it does not judge a school to be inadequate because of minor administrative errors, or because an inspector's ID was not checked. Ofsted does not try to 'catch schools out'."

Here, in summary form, are the findings of the Ofsted report. Most of the features of outstanding practice are found, to a greater or lesser extent, in all effective schools with outstanding safeguarding arrangements:
- High-quality leadership and management that makes safeguarding a

priority across all aspects of a school's work
• Stringent vetting procedures in place for staff and other adults
• Rigorous safeguarding policies and procedures in place, written in plain English, compliant with statutory requirements and updated regularly; in particular, clear and coherent child protection policies
• Child protection arrangements that are accessible to everyone, so that pupils and families, as well as adults in the school, know who they can talk to if they are worried
• Excellent communication systems with up-to-date information that can be accessed and shared by those who need it
• A high priority given to training in safeguarding, generally going beyond basic requirements, extending expertise widely and building internal capacity
• Robust arrangements for site security, understood and applied by staff and pupils
• A curriculum that is flexible, relevant and engages pupils' interest; that is used to promote safeguarding, not least through teaching pupils how to stay safe, how to protect themselves from harm and how to take responsibility for their own and others' safety
• Courteous and responsible behaviour by the pupils, enabling everyone to feel secure and well-protected
• Well thought out and workable day-to-day arrangements to protect and promote pupils' health and safety
• Rigorous monitoring of absence, with timely and appropriate follow-up, to ensure that pupils attend regularly
• Risk assessment taken seriously and used to good effect in promoting safety.

Digital Infrastructure

In 2006, Christine Gilbert wrote to the then secretary of state for education on behalf of the Teaching and Learning 2020 Review Group outlining what teaching and learning might look like in our schools in the year 2020. Hard to believe that we are now fast approaching that futuristic time.

Gilbert's report outlined what schools needed to do if they were to meet the needs of young people in the 21st Century. She talked about the need to personalise learning by "focusing in a more structured way on each child's learning in order to enhance progress, achievement and participation".

The review group set out what they saw as the main drivers of change – the five things they said would drive major changes in society and, therefore,

five foci for schools to take account of between 2006 and 2020. These drivers were:
1. Demographic
2. Social
3. Technological
4. Economic
5. Environmental

One of the key drivers of change, the report said, was technology: the group predicted that using ICT would be natural for most students and for most teachers by 2020. It also predicted that the economy would be knowledge-based. At their heart, all five 'drivers' are concerned with technology: technology is changing the world students will inhabit; and technology is changing the way students learn in order to be prepared for this new world.

The report said that:

"Our vision is one in which these aspirations are realised for all children and young people. The education system will need to act now if it is to transform the experience of children starting school today. We do not underestimate the challenges involved. However, we believe that the process of achieving our vision will be an exciting one in which many schools are already leading the way.

"Together, schools, local and national government need to work towards a society in which:
- A child's chances of success are not related to his or her socio-economic background, gender or ethnicity
- Education services are designed around the needs of each child, with the expectation that all learners achieve high standards
- All children and young people leave school with functional skills in English and mathematics, understanding how to learn, think creatively, take risks and handle change
- Teachers use their skills and knowledge to engage children and young people as partners in learning, acting quickly to adjust their teaching in response to pupils' learning
- Schools draw in parents as their child's co-educators, engaging them and increasing their capacity to support their child's learning.

"We believe that personalising learning and teaching must play a central role in transforming England's education service to achieve these aims between now and 2020."

The report places significant weight on the part that new technologies have to play in realising this 20:20 vision. It says:

"Already, with significant government investment, over the past ten years the use of technology in schools has increased considerably. The new technologies have an impact on a school in three main areas:
- The administration of the school, including budgeting, planning and databases managing pupil details and progress
- The creation and delivery of lesson materials, including teachers' and pupils' use of whiteboards, visualisers, handheld voting devices and tablet PCs to enable reproduction of and access to resources
- The use of domestic digital technology as a learning tool, including home access to the internet, digital cameras, video cameras, gaming devices, Personal Digital Assistants (PDAs) and mobile phones.

"New technologies," the report continues, "contribute to personalising learning by influencing what, how and why children learn" by:
- Broadening the range of learning material children are able to access, either guided by a teacher or as part of self-directed learning
- Enabling quick interactive assessments, for example, using 'voting' technology promoting development of a broad range of knowledge, skills and understanding, in new contexts and with virtual access to experts
- Facilitating collaboration with peers (in the same school and in other schools)
- Increasing the variety of learning resources, software and communication tools, through new media
- Helping schools to use a wider range of readily available resources and software to enhance learning, including making software available to children to use at home
- Blurring distinctions between informal and formal learning – giving children the ability to choose what they learn and when they learn it
- Increasing motivation, through pace and variety
- Increased relevance, through greater links between children's experience of school and of the technology-rich world outside.

And the success of ICT can, the report said, be supported by:
- Engagement with parents and pupils - expanding the potential for communication, sharing resources, creating shared spaces to record pupils' learning and progress
- Whole-school systems - integrated learning and management systems that bring together all the information on pupils' progress and analysis of assessment data, and are capable of being shared with other schools and

organisations

This report is now over a decade old and some of what it had to say on the subject of 21st Century skills are perhaps dubious. However, many of its predictions about the central role technology will play in schools and in the world of work are hard to argue.

What is particularly clear from reading the report and reviewing what has happened in schools in the ten years since its publication is that ICT is not just about supporting students' learning, it is also about supporting teachers and others to monitor and track student progress, as well as report to parents.

The report says that, "While all schools have systems for recording and reporting information about pupils and their achievement, this information is not always readily available to those who could draw on it to improve learning, namely classroom teachers, pupils, and parents. Using the new technologies to inform learning and teaching will be a priority. This should take advantage of the potential of on-line learning opportunities linked to individual learning plans (or 'e-portfolios') and information held on pupils' progress."

It follows, therefore, that ICT is a vital resource for school leaders to manage. But here is a word of caution…

Developing ICT in schools is often underestimated: it is assumed that using ICT simply means using an interactive whiteboard. All too often, schools take a single-minded approach to ICT - they assume effective ICT solely means teachers using ICT in lessons (and overusing new technologies); they view ICT as a panacea and use it every lesson. This has several negative effects: not least, 'death by Powerpoint'! If a new technology is over-used, students become apathetic towards it and are less engaged in their learning. If technology is used for the sake of it when more traditional means of teaching would be better, the key learning is lost amidst the 'light show'.

ICT is about much more than using interactive whiteboards or iPads in class. When used well, ICT can:
- Promote social interaction
- Support inclusion
- Provide a safe environment
- Enable students to track their own progress
- Enable parents to engage with school
- Motivate staff

- Enable teachers to create resources
- Support planning
- Support target-setting, assessment and reporting
- Support school improvement planning, and monitoring and reviewing performance
- Allow for efficient administration and reduce bureaucracy

ICT should be seen as a vital tool not just for teachers in the classroom but for the admin team, for middle and senior leaders, and for parents and governors. ICT shouldn't be viewed simply as a learning resource but should be seen as a means of improving efficiency and reducing bureaucracy. It should also be seen as a means of tracking student progress, of tracking school improvement, and of extending the boundaries of learning beyond the school gates.

If ICT is to be used effectively and in these diverse ways, school leaders should consider the following challenges when developing ICT in schools:

Safeguarding
How will your school ensure that children are protected and kept safe whilst using ICT?

Inclusion
How will your school ensure that the use of ICT is differentiated?

Good value for money
How will your school ensure that ICT is affordable and has long-term benefits?

Home access
How will your school ensure every student has fair access and that you extend the boundaries of learning for every child? How will you ensure parental engagement?

If we take these four items as our list of ICT challenges, our priorities for ICT development should, therefore, be:

1. Promoting student entitlement and encouraging the use of ICT for learning
2. universal – and safe – access in and out of school
3. Developing appropriate professional tools and providing training for staff
4. Developing a cost-effective, reliable digital infrastructure and having

in place effective contingency plans for when that infrastructure fails

School leaders, therefore, have the duty to manage the school's digital infrastructure. They should have a long-term vision for the way ICT is used in order to promote student progress and to reduce bureaucracy for staff. ICT should form part of the school improvement plan - as an objective in its own right and as a means of achieving other objectives.

CHAPTER SEVENTEEN
How can school leaders make effective use of Pupil Premium funding?

In Chapter Sixteen I explained that one source of significant income for schools is the Pupil Premium Grant.

The Pupil Premium is money given to schools to help disadvantaged students.

One in four children in the UK grows up in poverty. The attainment gap between rich and poor is detectable from as early as 22 months and continues to widen throughout the education system. Children from the lowest income homes are half as likely to get five good GCSEs and go on to higher education as the national average. White working class students (particularly boys) are amongst the lowest performers. The link between poverty and attainment is multi-racial.

The effective use of Pupil Premium funding is an essential weapon in a school's armoury in the battle to close the attainment gap between disadvantaged students and their non-disadvantaged peers and is a key consideration for school leaders. So how can you ensure that you're making best use of your school's money and demonstrating its impact? How can you ensure that the progress of every one of your students who's in receipt of the funding is monitored and that interventions are put into place in a timely manner as soon as their progress falters? And how can you be sure that those interventions are the most effective strategies you can use and offer the best value for money for the public purse? We will answer all of these questions and more in this chapter but before we look at how the Pupil Premium might best be utilised and how to report on its impact, let's first be clear about who the funding is for and how it can legally be spent...

Pupil Premium funding is awarded to students who are categorised as 'Ever

6 FSM'. In any given academic year, the funding is given to students who are recorded in the January school census and are known to have been eligible for free school meals (FSM) in any of the previous six years, as well as those first known to be eligible in January.

Pupil Premium funding is also awarded to students who are adopted from care or who have left care. The funding will be given to students who are recorded in the January school census and alternative provision census and who were looked after by an English or Welsh local authority immediately before being adopted, or who left local authority care on a special guardianship order or child arrangements order (previously known as a residence order).

Finally, Pupil Premium funding is awarded to students who are categorised as 'Ever 5 service child' which - for the purposes of the Pupil Premium grant conditions - means a student recorded in the January school census who was eligible for the service child premium in any of the previous four years as well as those recorded as a service child for the first time on the January school census.

Pupil Premium is for the purposes of the school it is awarded to. In other words, it is for the educational benefit of students registered at the school which is in receipt of the money. But it can also be used for the benefit of students registered at other maintained schools or academies and on community facilities such as services whose provision furthers any charitable purpose for the benefit of students at the school or their families, or people who live or work in the locality in which the school is situated. The money does not have to be completely spent by schools in the financial year it is awarded; some or all of it may be carried forward to future financial years.

Schools are held to account for how they spend the money and the impact that money has on closing the gap. For example, Ofsted inspections report on how a school's use of the funding affects the attainment of their disadvantaged students and the DfE holds a school to account through performance tables, which include data on the attainment of students who attract the funding, the progress made by these students, and the gap in attainment between disadvantaged students and their peers.

Ofsted's Common Inspection Handbook (2015) explains that when judging the effectiveness of leadership and management, inspectors will consider: "How effectively leaders use additional funding, including the Pupil Premium, and measure its impact on outcomes for pupils, and how effectively governors hold them to account for this."

The Pupil Premium is also mentioned in the grade descriptors for leadership and management. The 'outstanding' grade descriptors, for example, include the following: "Governors systematically challenge senior leaders so that the effective deployment of staff and resources, including the pupil premium and special educational needs (SEN) funding, secures excellent outcomes for pupils. Governors do not shy away from challenging leaders about variations in outcomes for pupil groups, especially between disadvantaged and other pupils." In the 'good' grade descriptors, meanwhile, it says: "Governors hold senior leaders stringently to account for all aspects of the school's performance, including the use of pupil premium and SEN funding, ensuring that the skilful deployment of staff and resources delivers good or improving outcomes for pupils."

When preparing for an inspection, the lead inspector will analyse information on the school's website, including its statement on the use of the Pupil Premium. The lead inspector will also request that any reports following an external review of the school's use of the Pupil Premium are made available at the start of the inspection. During the inspection, inspectors will gather evidence about the use of the Pupil Premium in relation to the following: The level of Pupil Premium funding received by the school that academic year and in previous years; how the school has spent the money and why it has decided to spend it in the way it has; and any differences made to the learning and progress of disadvantaged students as shown by outcomes data and inspection evidence.

Inspectors will take particular account of the progress made by disadvantaged students by the end of the key stage compared with that made nationally by other students with similar starting points and the extent to which any gaps in this progress, and consequently in attainment, are closing. Inspectors will compare the progress and attainment of the school's disadvantaged students with the national figures for the progress and attainment of non-disadvantaged students. They will then consider in-school gaps between disadvantaged and non-disadvantaged students, and how much these gaps are closing. Inspectors will consider in-school gaps between disadvantaged and non-disadvantaged students.

It's worth noting that inspectors are likely to compare the progress of disadvantaged students with all non-disadvantaged students, not just with those who have similar starting points because if inspectors only compared the progress and attainment of students who started at a similar level, they would be unable to establish if gaps in attainment between disadvantaged and non-disadvantaged students were closing.

Inspectors will check that the reason the gap is narrowing is because the attainment and progress of disadvantaged students is rising, rather than that of non-disadvantaged students falling. If an attainment gap exists or widens, inspectors will also consider whether this is because disadvantaged students attain more highly than others do nationally, but non-disadvantaged students in the school attain even more highly. The Common Inspection Framework says "these circumstances would not reflect negatively on the school".

In light of all this, I would recommend that school leaders prepare for any inspection or government visit by asking themselves the following questions:

1. Did I focus sufficiently on literacy and numeracy interventions?
2. Did I work with primary feeders to identify students who might benefit from summer schools, nurture groups, etc.?
3. Did I target my best teachers at my most disadvantaged students?
4. Did I apply for top-up summer school funding when it was available? (It was removed in 2016.)
5. Do all my teachers know who was eligible for Pupil Premium funding? Do they and governors know how that funding was used and what impact it has had?
6. Where do students do their homework and independent study? If they live in chaotic homes, do we provide a quiet space with support? Have I involved parents in making sure students use it?
7. What happened after I looked at the data? What interventions did it lead to and what was their impact? What have I learnt?
8. Did I have gaps between exclusion and attendance rates as well as attainment gaps?
9. Was a senior leader at my school responsible for Pupil Premium funding? Do we also have a governor responsible for it?
10. Did higher (and lower) attaining students make as much progress as non-FSM? (Remember, the Pupil Premium is not just there to get students up to age related minimum expectations.)
11. What did I use as a benchmark when I compared our performance to other schools? (Don't just compare FSM students to other FSM students; and look beyond local authority figures to national standards.)
12. How did I evaluate pastoral interventions? Did I ensure that, ultimately, they led to academic improvements as well as improvements in, say, attendance and behaviour?
13. When did I review my interventions? Did I track, review and

improve our provision as I went along rather than wait until the end?

The answers to these questions can provide the basis for your Pupil Premium action plan. So ask yourself: What do you need to do now in order to be fully prepared for inspection? Above all, as you prepare for inspection, remember this mantra: know thy impact!

Good practice

As you start working towards your action plan, what should you be aiming for? What's your end goal? What does good practice in this area look like?

Schools that use the Pupil Premium funding effectively and diminish the difference in the academic achievement of disadvantaged students compared to non-disadvantaged students tend to conduct a detailed analysis of where students are underachieving and why. They make good use of research evidence when choosing support and intervention activities but are discerning customers of research - they always contextualise the information, asking: How would this work in my school? And: What do I know already works in my context? Research is extremely valuable as a starting point but you must not underestimate your own knowledge of your school and its students and staff.

As well as applying research and personal knowledge, schools that use the Pupil Premium funding effectively tend to focus on high quality teaching rather than relying on interventions to compensate because they know that pedagogy trumps all - getting it right first time is the best approach and teaching matters more than curriculum. They ensure that their best teachers lead English and maths intervention groups. They make frequent use of achievement data in order to check the effectiveness of interventions and they do this early and continue to do it throughout the year rather than waiting until the intervention has finished and it's too late to change it.

These schools also tend to have a systematic focus on clear student feedback and students receive regular advice to help them improve their work. These schools have a designated senior leader with a clear overview of the funding allocation and a solid understanding of how the funding works and how it needs reporting. All the teachers in these schools are aware of the students who are eligible for Pupil Premium funding and they take responsibility for those students' progress. These schools have strategies in place for improving attendance, behaviour and links with families and communities if these are an issue, as well as for improving academic performance. And, finally, these schools ensure that the performance management of staff includes discussions about the Pupil Premium and about individual students in receipt of the funding and how they are progressing.

Common pitfalls

Conversely, in schools where the Pupil Premium isn't used effectively and is not tracked well enough, there tends to be a lack of clarity about the intended impact of interventions. These schools run the same intervention strategies year after year because that's just what they're used to doing or have the staff and resources for, irrespective of whether or not they work. There is no real monitoring of the quality and impact of the interventions and no real awareness of what works and what offers the best value for money. These schools also tend to spend the money indiscriminately on teaching assistants but teaching assistants are not well utilised.

The schools whose Pupil Premium practice is ineffective also tend to have an unclear audit trail and focus solely on students attaining the Level 4 benchmarks not higher. They tend to spend the Pupil Premium in isolation, it does not feature as part of the whole school development plan and decisions about it are not therefore taken in the round. These schools also compare their performance to local, not national, data. Pupil Premium funding is used for pastoral interventions but they are vague and not focused on desired outcomes for students. And, finally, in these schools, governors are not involved in taking decisions about Pupil Premium spending and are not informed about its use and impact.

What to report

Schools need to report on how much Pupil Premium funding they received in the current academic year and how they intend to spend the funding. They need to be able to articulate their reasons and evidence for this. Schools also need to report on how they spent the funding they received for the last academic year and what difference it made to the attainment of disadvantaged students.

The funding is allocated for each financial year, but the information schools publish online should refer to the academic year as this is how parents and the general public understand the school year. As schools won't know how much funding they're getting for the latter part of the academic year (from April to July), they should report on the funding up to the end of the financial year then update the information when they have all the data.

If the school receives Year 7 literacy and numeracy catch-up premium funding, they must also publish details of how they spend this funding and the effect this has had on the attainment of the students who attract it.

CHAPTER EIGHTEEN
What does an effective exams analysis look like?

In most schools, school leaders run exam analysis meetings in the autumn term in order to scrutinise and learn from the summer results. These exam analysis meetings go by many names, most of them aptly funereal in tone, such as 'post-mortems' or 'rapid improvement panels' (RIPs).

One by one, middle leaders step forward, heads bowed reverently, to get a grilling from a grim reaper in the guise of senior leaders, academy sponsors, school governors and headteachers/principals who form part of the post-exam review panel.

The primary purpose of these meetings is to interrogate a school's summative performance data, celebrating success where it occurs (recognising departmental improvements as well as individual accomplishments) and questioning underperformance or significant deviations from predicated outcomes in the hope that the same mistakes can be avoided next year.

School leaders should prepare their data analysis reports in advance of the panel meeting and submit it to the panel for their consideration. Panellists should interrogate the report, highlighting key strengths and weaknesses, and annotating pertinent questions and concerns. This will allow the meeting itself to focus on panellists' questions rather than leaders' presentations in order to try to ascertain more fully the reasons for certain outcomes and trends. There is no doubt that leaders can present their findings in a positive light, but what is needed is an honest account of the facts and an appropriate level of challenge, leading to an agreed set of SMART actions rather than vague promises.

Exam analysis reports should not be too long or descriptive. Rather, they should be succinct and evaluative in nature. Panellists want to know the following:

- What are the headline results per subject per year group and per cohort/class?
- What was attainment like versus what was predicted?
- What was attainment like versus what was targeted/expected?
- What was progress like versus what was predicted?
- What was progress like versus what was targeted/expected?
- What value did each teacher add (often presented in terms of residual scores where any positive figure shows value was added)?
- How did different groups of students attain and progress in relation to all students, including boys and girls, students in receipt of Pupil Premium funding, students for whom English is an additional language, students with SEND, and so on?
- What interventions were put in place, when and for which students?
- What effect did each intervention have, what has been learnt about the value of each intervention?
- What was the accuracy and quality of teacher assessment like?

Once all these meetings have been concluded, the headteacher/principal must collate and summarise the school's performance in order to present it to the governing body, academy sponsors or executive principal. At this stage it is worth a headteacher/principal remembering that exam results are exactly that: results. They exist in the past tense and cannot be improved (with the exception of exam papers which are entered for remarks, of course; though under recent reforms this practice will become less common). The only point of an exam post-mortem is to ascertain the 'cause of death', so to speak, so that appropriate action can be taken in the future in order to benefit the living.

As such, what a school's stakeholders really want to know while they're reviewing exam results is what led to those results: what worked and what didn't; what lessons have been or can now be learnt. Accordingly, here is some advice for headteachers/principals and senior leaders who expect to face inquisitions from their executive heads, sponsors and governors…

1. *Present your data clearly, succinctly and honestly.*
Don't try to mask your data by combining various qualifications. Although it might feel like it, it is not a witch-hunt and you will gain nothing by being in denial or being defensive. Moreover, you will fool no one by massaging your data.

2. *Keep track of which interventions are given to which students and*

analyse their relative effectiveness in light of the outcomes.
You need to demonstrate value for money, so must evaluate the relative success of all your intervention strategies. This is not always easy but, in the case of the Pupil Premium in particular, it is important that you try because Ofsted and the DfE expect to see evidence of successful use of the Pupil Premium. Where you know a student has only been in receipt of one form of intervention, use him or her as a test base to compare the effectiveness of that strategy versus another.

3. Identify which teachers achieved the highest value added scores/high grade achievements.
Decide how to employ your best teachers this year. This isn't always necessarily with the top set or the C/D borderline class, especially now we have a 1–9 grading system and a focus on the progress of the majority not the attainment of the minority. Think creatively about each teacher's particular skill-set, try to 'think outside the box' a little.

4. Analyse how accurate your internal moderation proved to be.
What more could be done to ensure that your teachers mark coursework and/or controlled assessments accurately? Also, analyse how accurately your teachers predicted their students' outcomes and carry out a question-by-question analysis of the exam. Which questions proved the most difficult for students? What more can you do this year to better prepare students for that question? What support do your teachers need to help them teach those aspects of the syllabus better? Ensure that all this self-flagellation leads to clear and SMART actions against which you and your staff can be held to account.

5. What professional development do your teachers need to help them improve?
What other actions need to be taken to improve the performance of your team? Do any formal procedures now need to be invoked in order to tackle endemic underperformance or malpractice? Did you, as the headteacher/senior leader, challenge your senior and middle leaders and their teachers? Did you do everything you could to keep track of the progress of every student and take appropriate actions to intervene when it was needed?

When presenting to governors or academy trust board members, you should aim for a balance between honest self-reflection and dogged determination to drive up standards. Be proud of your school and your staff and don't be afraid to sing the praises of those who deserve it. But also be frank about failure where it exists and have a robust plan to tackle it.

Your key focus at all times must be on:

Impact:
What was the impact of the actions you took last year on student outcomes and what did that teach you?

Action:
What SMART actions will you take this year in order to improve student outcomes and what will the impact of those actions be next summer when you face the grim reaper again?

CHAPTER NINETEEN
How can school leaders work productively with governors?

Naturally, the model of governance employed at your school depends on the type of school you work in. Some schools are controlled by the local authority; others are controlled by a diocese or by sponsors; new 'free schools' are controlled by myriad groups of interested persons including parents and media personalities. But, whatever type of school you work in, it is likely to have a local governing body (or LGB).

The relationship between the senior team and the governing body is vital if a school is to become outstanding. School leaders need to understand the role of the governing body and governors need to appreciate what they are and are not permitted to do. The lines need to be drawn. A simple rule of thumb when demarcating roles and responsibilities is this:

- Governors are concerned with strategy
- School leaders are concerned with leadership and management

But school governance is an odd thing: the distinction between school leaders and governors can easily become blurred; it is not always clear where the real power lies, and where support and challenge cross over into direction and command. Some governing bodies are passive and trust their headteacher/principal and senior team to run the school how they see fit, relying on the local authority to provide the appropriate checks and balances. Other governing bodies are active and hold the headteacher/principal and senior team firmly to account; they scrutinise every decision and pore over performance data and the school budget with keen eyes.

The lines have become ever more blurred since Ofsted published its last Common Inspection Framework in 2015. Many of the descriptors under the heading 'leadership and management' now refer to 'leaders, managers and governors'. The message is clear: governors are now expected to be involved in, not just informed about, the decisions taken in school. This is particularly true of decisions about how to spend the Pupil Premium Grant (PPG) and about how to manage the educational provision of different groups of students including those with special educational needs and disabilities (SEND).

My own view is this: governors are akin to a board of non-executive directors in a company - they work for the school and should be champions of it, speaking highly of the school within the local community and protecting its best interests; governors are not independent arbiters or representatives of community interests or constituents.

It is true that governing bodies exist to provide strategic leadership and to be the accountable body. It's also true, therefore, that they need to be able to support and challenge the senior team's decisions. To do this, they need to be kept informed and they need to understand where the school is going. They need to know that the information with which they are supplied is honest and accurate. There is nothing to be gained by headteachers/principals 'massaging' the data or providing redacted information.

But governors' challenges should not extend to public criticisms of the school. It is not uncommon for a chair of governors and headteacher/principal to disagree over key decisions and for there to ensue a robust, often bitter, dispute. These disputes are not always entirely unhealthy, either. A headteacher/principal needs challenge and if his or her decision can not be justified to the chair of governors then it is just possible that it is a bad decision. Good or bad, decisions are always better when subject to scrutiny.

Equally, a headteacher/principal should be able to question the governing body's decisions and/or perceptions and make them see the reality of a situation. It is the head, not the governors, who works in the school every day and has the better understanding of what works and what does not work. It is the head, not the governors, who knows his or her staff best and has a duty of care towards them. But disagreements between a headteacher/principal and a chair of governors should be kept private - private from the community and private from other school staff - because it is important for morale that governors and senior leaders are seen to have one voice, are seen to be working in unison. Public disagreements or disparaging remarks by governors can be damaging not only to the school's reputation but also to staff morale - which, in turn, could hamper performance and therefore be a self-fulfilling prophecy.

It is equally important that the headteacher/principal respects his governing body and involves governors in key decision-making. It is also important that he or she keeps his governing body informed on a regular basis - not least because this is something Ofsted look for. In the new inspection framework, as I have indicated, governance is consumed within the overall leadership and management judgment and so no matter how effective the senior team is, the school cannot be judged good or outstanding for leadership and management if its governing body is not genuinely involved and regularly informed.

And I say all of the above as a former headteacher and as a current school governor. I have been on a number of governing bodies at primary and secondary level, and also worked closely with the governing body of a large further education college. I have been on both sides of the boardroom table and understand the frustrations on each side.

*

What is the governing body's role?

Governors are about strategy and need to work with senior leaders on agreeing the school's direction of travel, on agreeing the school's priorities going forward, and on agreeing the key objectives in the school improvement plan.

In particular, governors are responsible for the strategic leadership of:
- School finances
- Staffing and personnel (including appointing new staff, reorganising and restructuring existing staff such as reassigning leadership responsibilities)
- Discipline and pastoral care
- The performance management of the headteacher/principal
- The curriculum plan
- Provision for students with SEND
- Provision for disadvantaged students including those in receipt of the Pupil Premium
- School buildings and their environment (including health and safety, and safeguarding and child protection)
- The school admissions policy and enrolment decisions
- Target-setting and assessment procedures, including reporting to parents

- The school self-evaluation form (SEF)
- The school improvement plan (SIP)
- Other aspects of school self-evaluation at all levels, including through governor link visits

Governors are not about day-to-day management: this remains the responsibility of the senior team and other school personnel.

It is important that senior leaders and governors support and respect each other and empathise with each other's roles. Senior leaders should never forget that (in most cases, though the government is considering changes to this) governors are unpaid volunteers who dedicate a lot of their own time to helping the school and they do so because they genuinely care about the school and about the young people in its care. Equally, governors should never forget that senior leaders are paid to take difficult decisions and are appointed on the basis that they have demonstrated the capacity and ability to lead a school. Accordingly, they should be afforded the time and space to lead the school effectively. If they are not afforded this time and space, then they cannot be held to account for the consequences of their actions or for the performance of their school.

This delicate balance is best struck through a clarity of procedures and policies. Systems and structures need to be in place to make clear everybody's roles and to ensure everybody performs those roles effectively or is appropriately challenged if they fall short of what is expected of them.

Senior leaders should develop good working relationships with governors, especially the chairs of the various governors' committees (if indeed the governing body runs a committee structure) through which important information can be fed.

Link governors should also act as conduits of information and as such they need to develop effective working relationships with their link middle and senior leaders, relationships based on mutual respect and trust. Link governors for some areas may need to make regular contact and be voracious in challenging their link member of staff for his or her decisions and actions; other link governors - secure in the improvements made by their link member of staff and by that person's knowledge, skills and experience - can step back and need only provide support when it is asked for.

Senior leaders should also provide key briefing documents to governors in order to assist governors in making important strategic decisions: this can best be achieved by leaders providing high quality summaries or headline data (not long, detailed reports) and a set of reasoned options for governors to debate and decide upon. These documents should be distributed in advance of decision-making meetings to allow thoughtful consideration and to avoid protracted discussions.

In addition to providing strategic leadership to those areas of school listed above, governors are also responsible for the following ongoing tasks:

Monitoring the school improvement plan
This can be done through the headteacher's/principal's report, through discussions at governors' meetings and/or via reports and data analysis from school leaders including heads of department.

Visiting the school
Visits are likely to be made at key times such as during interviews, appraisals, and at times of uncertainty and change; governors are also likely to visit the school to attend important events such as presentations and open evenings.

Attending link meetings
Governors are likely to be linked to the curriculum, pastoral or admin areas for which they are accountable and should meet with their link contact at key points in the year (though, as I say above, the nature and frequency of such visits should be tailored to suit the context: some departments need a 'light touch' because they are thriving - such visits might therefore be about recognising and celebrating achievement; others might need closer attention).

The key to an effective working relationship between senior leaders and the governing body is for both parties to be open and honest and to keep the other informed. As I said earlier, there is nothing to be gained by keeping secrets or by being duplicitous. Both parties should also remember that they are on the same side and should find ways of working together for the benefit of the school.

In situations where the headteacher/principal and chair of governors struggle to build an effective working relationship, it is important that both parties remain professional. Heads also need to recognise that the government has given governors a more formal role which might not suit what the head wants or is used to.

It may be necessary to bring in a critical friend, someone who will mediate a conversation between the headteacher/principal and either the chair of governors or the whole governing body. One strategy the critical friend could employ is to carry out a governors' self-review exercise to look at what's working well and what could be improved about the way the governing body works. This may help bring issues out into the open in a 'safe' way. It may also be useful for the critical friend to write down sets of expectations for both sides, to talk through them so that, in the end, there are no unfounded assumptions being made on either side about what each can expect. Furthermore, policies, procedures and an agreed code of conduct can help ensure that everyone abides by the same rules.

CHAPTER TWENTY
How can school leaders engage parents?

I have heard it said that parents are a school's customers. I disagree with this analogy. The relationship between a school and its students' parents is much more complex than that which exists between a company and its customers. Yes, a school provides a service to its parents but that service is one of the most important services imaginable: that of securing a good future for their sons and daughters. Indeed, what could be more important - other than a child's health - than a child's education. But schools are not beholden to parents, they do not exist to serve parents. Often a school knows better than a parent what is in the best interests of the student (and I am speaking as a father of three). Often a school has to challenge and question a parent's behaviour or beliefs. Often a school has to say difficult and unpopular things or refer a parent to the police or social services. No, the relationship between a school and its parents is more complex than that.

The relationship between schools and parents - however we wish to describe or define it - should be built on mutual trust and respect but this can often be hard-fought. The best starting point for school leaders when forging this relationship is to consider how their school is going to engage with parents.

School leaders should always stay calm and talk quietly to parents. Sometimes it may be necessary to remove a parent from a place of conflict. It is important that school leaders remember that they are a role model - the professional - and should lead by example. Accordingly, they should not respond to a parent's aggression by raising their voices nor should they be intimidated by foul language.

School leaders are gatekeepers for their staff: they should protect their staff and should not let a parent see a teacher until there is a reduction in the aggression (and even then it may not be the best course of action). It is worth adopting a clear policy regarding meetings with teachers which has the following caveat at its heart: a teacher's first duty is to teach his or her classes and not to meet with parents; appointments, therefore, have to be arranged in advance and parents without prior appointments will not be seen. Instead of referring parents to the classroom teacher, senior leaders should listen to the parent personally (when the parent has become calm) and note the nature of the complaint.

They should allow the parent a reasonable amount of time to articulate their grievance and should avoid interrupting because this may aggravate the situation further. Of course, this has to be balanced with the senior leader's need to utilise their own time effectively and perform their other duties. Once they have listened, they should summarise the key points as they understand them and ask for clarification on any points of confusion. Then they should promise to gather together all the information they will need in order to make a comprehensive and fair assessment of the matter.

Senior leaders should not immediately side with or agree with the parent or the teacher. Nor should they promise any specific action. Rather, they should promise to phone or meet with the parent again at an agreed time - ideally within a couple of days - in order to take the matter forward. The school leader should then investigate the circumstances with the appropriate members of staff, look for a fair and just solution and see how both parties can be brought together to resolve the matter.

Any action should be taken with the best interests of the school in mind: the right decision for the majority of students may not be what the parent wants you to do, nor what the teacher wants you to do. You should be confident that you are taking the right decision in the circumstances and once all the facts are known, and you should be confident that your decision will stand up to scrutiny over the long-term. Of course, depending on the severity of the incident, it may be advisable to consult with other senior colleagues or your headteacher/principal or, if you are the headteacher, your executive principal, chair of governors of trust board member, or, for maintained schools, a local authority advisor.

In order to avoid confrontation from arising in the first place, your school should have a clear policy for dealing with parents which is known and understood by all parents. But avoiding conflict is not the only reason for having a parental engagement policy. Indeed, being clear about how often and in what forms you communicate with parents will also help you to work productively with parents on improving all aspects of a student's experience of and interaction with school.

In fact, parental engagement is of great import in all sorts of ways...

According to Butler et el (2008), Haynes et al (1989), and Henderson (1987), for example, it is associated with higher academic achievement. Butler and Haynes also claim that effective parental engagement leads to increased rates of student attendance. Becher (1984) and Henderson et al (1986) say it can have a positive effect on students' attitudes to learning and on their behaviour.

Research has also shown that getting a school's communications policy right can lead to an increased level of interest amongst students in their work (see, for example, Rich [1988] and Tobolka [2006]), increased parent satisfaction with their child's teachers (Rich), and higher rates of teacher satisfaction (MetLife [2012]).

So what should your school's parental engagement policy look like? Firstly, it should set out what you expect parents to do. For example...

> *We encourage parents to:*
> - *Be supportive,*
> - *Be informed,*
> - *Maintain a direct involvement in their child's progress,*
> - *Understand what the school is trying to achieve for their child,*
> - *Take a positive position - contribute to initiatives like home visits and information-gathering events such as parents' consultation evenings,*
> - *Visit school and be informed about issues and initiatives,*
> - *Support events that promote the school efforts,*
> - *Be aware of and support any home/school agreements.*

Your parental engagement policy should also outline how your school intends to communicate with parents and how it will consult with parents on key decisions. It may be useful to start with a statement of intent such as this:

> *Our school, in order to be effective, must acknowledge, appreciate and respond to the views of parents. It needs to take informed decisions following consultation processes.*

Your school will communicate with parents in a variety of ways including:
- Parents' consultation evenings
- Open evenings
- Information meetings
- Parents' workshops and discussion forums

- Parents' associations or committees
- Formal questionnaires and market research products
- Regular newsletters
- The school website
- Online reporting and the parents' portal
- Text messaging
- Email

Your school will need a clear strategy for communicating effectively and expediently in each of these circumstances.

As well as writing letters (your school should have a policy dictating your 'house style' and letters should be checked and formatted by the admin team), it is likely you will use email and text messaging to communicate with parents. Before relying on email and texts to impart important information, it is vital you understand access arrangements: do all parents have internet and mobile phone coverage and do all parents have the financial means to utilise it? Will you disadvantage some parents if you rely solely on email and texts? You may need to adopt a 'belt and braces' approach to communication by sending a text and/or email to indicate that a letter is on its way.

And what of the school website? Your school should have a policy explaining how it will use its website to aid communication. It is likely it will be used for publishing news articles, celebrating school successes and reproducing the school calendar. It may also - and to be an outstanding school which extends the boundaries of learning, it should - use the website for setting work and for providing help and advice to students. The website may provide an overview of each course and syllabus being taught in school and may have links to homework tasks and extension tasks should students and parents wish to do extra work in order to secure the learning or to revise.

As well as a policy for how your school communicates with parents, it will need a policy for how staff use these means of communication to ensure accuracy, timeliness and appropriateness.

*

Here are some other tips for improving the effectiveness of your communications with parents…

Firstly, communication needs to start early and continue throughout a student's journey through school. The parents of students moving from nursery to primary school, or from primary to secondary, will not want to receive information halfway through the summer holiday at which point it will be deemed too late. Schools need to engage with parents early and clearly set out their expectations and requirements.

Secondly, communication needs to be a two-way process: as well as the school staying in touch with parents, parents also need a means of keeping in contact with the school. One way to do this is to create a frequently asked questions (FAQ) page, as well as a Q&A facility and a parents' forum on the school's website. This will need to be monitored carefully, of course, or perhaps pass through a 'gatekeeper' in order to be vetted before comments are made 'live'. In order for it to be viewed as worthwhile, the school will also need to communicate its response to parental comments and suggestions, perhaps through a 'You Said, We Did' page.

Thirdly, communications need to be appropriately timed, relevant and useful and one way to do this is to utilise the experience and expertise of students and their parents. For example, the parents of current Reception or Year 7 students will be able to share their thoughts on what information they needed when they went through the transition process with their child not so long ago, as well as when they needed it most, whilst current Reception or Year 7 students will be able to offer their advice about how to prepare for primary or secondary school by, to give but two examples, providing a reading list for the summer and sharing their advice on how to get ready for the first day of school.

Fourthly, parental communication should take many forms and embrace new and emerging technologies. The use of technologies such as email, texting, websites, electronic portfolios and online assessment and reporting tools have - accordingly to Merkley, Schmidt, Dirksen and Fuhler (2006) - made communication between parents and teachers more timely, efficient, productive and satisfying.

So what might this look like in practice? Here are a few suggestions for how technology, for example, could be used to help a school communicate with parents and vice versa…

Parents could send teachers an email to let them know when the home learning environment may be (temporarily or otherwise) holding a student back.

Likewise, teachers could send parents an email to let them know when issues arise at school which may have a detrimental effect on the student, such as noticeable changes in behaviour or deficits in academic performance.

Teachers could text parents at the end of the day on which a student has done something particularly well or shown real progress or promise. Instant and personal feedback like this is really valuable and helps make a connection between the teacher and the parents.

Teachers could send half-termly or monthly newsletters via email to parents to inform them about what topics they are covering in class in the coming weeks, what homework will be set and when, and how parents can help.

The school could use text, email and the school website to keep parents updated on forthcoming field trips, parent association meetings and other school activities.

Teachers could use email to send out regular tips to parents on how they might be able to support their child's learning that week/month. For example, they could send a list of questions to ask their child about what students have been learning in class. They could also send hyperlinks to interactive quizzes or games.

The school could use the school website to gather more frequent and informal parent voice information about specific topics. For example, they might post a short survey after each open evening and parents' evening.

The school could provide an online calendar via its website to allow parents to volunteer to help in class, say as reading mentors, or at special events.

An online calendar could also be used as a booking facility to enable parents to make their own meetings with school staff rather than having to phone the school, which many people find daunting.

Finally, the online calendar could prove useful for booking slots at parents' evenings and other open evenings and events, enabling parents to be in control of the times at which they attend school rather than relying on a child and their teachers to agree suitable slots.

Even once a school has established and embedded an effective parental engagement strategy, some parents are likely to remain hard to reach and it's often these parents that a school needs to engage with the most. So why do some parents find it difficult to talk to their child's school?

Sometimes it's because they lead busy, complicated lives and schools don't often present themselves as being high on their to-do list. Also, school's operating hours tend to clash with parents' working lives. Other times, it's because a parent had a difficult experience of school as a youngster and remains reluctant to enter a school building or talk with teachers. They may be daunted and even afraid. In both these cases, a school may need to consider alternative approaches, such as engaging with parents by telephone in the evenings and weekends, or meeting with them at another - neutral - location nearby, perhaps even using a 'go-between' such as another parent who is known to be engaged and reliable.

Some parents may have poor levels of literacy and so will need to be communicated with more sensitively in order that they do not misunderstand the nature and purpose of the communication, and in order to make it easier for them to respond without fear of humiliation.

Hard-to-reach parents are often the parents that schools need to reach most because their children - as a result of a lack of involvement or interest at home - attend school infrequently or late, present behavioural challenges when they do attend, and/or have low levels of literacy and/or numeracy.

Where parents have consistently condoned their child's absence from school, there is much to be done in establishing and developing positive relationships between the school and the parents, and in educating parents on the impact of poor attendance.

The appointment of a specialist, such as a home-school liaison officer, may prove a successful approach where schools need to improve achievement in the longer term.

Much depends on building up and sustaining positive relationships between parents and the school. The introduction of rewards and incentives (that are also seen as being attractive to students) can help promote improved attendance, behaviour and achievement. Parents will have their own views about such reward schemes and should be consulted.

Some parents are hard to reach because they are newly arrived in the UK, have nascent (or no) English skills, and feel alienated from society and schools. Moreover, language and cultural differences can make parents feel intimidated by schools. It's also possible that some parents emigrated from a country where parental involvement in their child's school was actively discouraged, and their re-education in the ways of English schooling may prove a significant barrier for them.

One solution to this challenge is to arrange for a mother-tongue speaker to meet with parents, offering classes in English language and/or offering induction sessions to help parents become more familiar with and confident in their understanding of the school system in the UK. This works both ways, of course.... A school may also benefit from arranging information sessions run by recently-immigrated parents and aimed at helping school staff to gain a better understanding of the lifestyles, traditions and customs of local ethnic minority groups.

CHAPTER TWENTY-ONE
What does effective community cohesion look like?

In Chapter One I state that senior leaders should develop and encourage effective partnerships with other schools, agencies and the community. I also opine that community cohesion is frequently misunderstood or underestimated: it is solely seen as being about offering the school site to the local community. And, yes, encouraging community use of your school is important (be it leasing your fields to the local football team or running adult education classes in the evenings). But community cohesion is also about respecting diversity and protecting vulnerable learners; it is about better understanding the local community and taking account of where students come from; it is about working with parents; it is about bringing world issues into schools in order to raise students' awareness of the world around them; it is about responding to the Prevent agenda and promoting fundamental British values,; and it is respecting diversity and inclusion of all types, ensuring every child has the opportunity to fulfil his or her potential irrespective of where they come from and what means they have.

Community cohesion, therefore, is about:
• Tracking vulnerable groups to ensure all students make good progress
• Using the school for community events
• Developing an international dimension through exchange programmes or special events
• Developing an effective inclusion policy which includes arrangements for student induction

Why? Because community cohesion is strongest when:

• Systems for student tracking ensure that student progress is carefully monitored for all groups of learners including vulnerable students such as those on free school meals, those with special educational needs and those from ethnic minorities or challenging backgrounds;

- The school is seen as a community hub and the community feels a part of the school - it is committed to helping the school to improve and celebrates its successes;

- There is some sort of international dimension to the work of the school which informs students about what is happening in the world around them, and encourages them to be more understanding and empathetic towards other cultures;

- There is an effective inclusion policy which promotes genuine inclusivity for all students and there is an appropriate induction process for new students and their families which makes them feel welcome, makes them feel a part of the school 'family' and makes them feel able to contribute to school life.

A school should actively seek partnerships with its community in order to provide enrichment opportunities. For example, partnerships with local businesses might open doors to school trips and work experience placements. It might also encourage local business leaders and entrepreneurs to visit school to give talks or to assist with mock interviews and CV writing workshops. Schools should encourage community leaders to attend and contribute to school events on a regular basis, perhaps they could award prizes at presentation evenings and in assemblies.

The school, in turn, should endeavour to make a contribution to community groups that support vulnerable people, and the school should support the wider community through charitable activities and fund-raising events. Perhaps the school could become involved in a community project.

Schools should involve their local community in their work by keeping them informed about school events and successes through newsletters, the local media, and their web site. They should invest time and thought into how they market their successes within the community because to do so is vital to raising the school's profile.

Raising the school's profile is, in turn, vital to making the school an attractive proposition to new students and families, and to ensuring it remains highly thought of. And, as I say in the introduction, message is important. Controlling the message certainly helps a school to market itself to prospective students and their parents and, through this, it helps a school to be oversubscribed and financially viable.

CHAPTER TWENTY-TWO
What kind of school leader is the most successful?

"The strength of a nation's economy and the vitality of its society depend on the quality of its schools..." So begins a report by the Centre for High Performance (published in the Harvard Business Review in 2017) on what makes a school leader successful. The study, by researchers Ben Laker and Alex Hill, which examined 411 school leaders working in 160 academy schools in England, concluded that the system was appointing, recognising and rewarding the wrong kind of school leader.

The report posited five types of leader but found that the most effective - the leaders who turned around failing schools and built institutions in which exam results improved year-on-year and continued to improve long after they'd left - were the least well-known, the least recognised, and the least rewarded.

Before we consider which kind of leader is the most successful and why, let's examine all five types...

1. **Surgeons** - these leaders cut and redirect, and focus on test scores.

1. Surgeons - these leaders cut and redirect, and focus on test scores.

Surgeons are both decisive and incisive; they quickly identify what's not working and redirect resources to the most pressing problems - how to improve this year's exam results. 85% of the 'surgeons' in the study were PE or RS teachers who had a high profile both inside and outside their school. They believed schools failed because students were not performing and if they removed the poor performers and made the rest work harder, performance would improve.

Surgeons are tough, disciplined leaders who focus on investing in the oldest students as these are the ones about to take their exams, often at the expense of anything and anyone else. They move the best teachers into exam years, reduce class sizes and increase interventions such as revision classes.

2. **Soldiers** - these leaders trim and tighten, and focus on the bottom line.

2. Soldiers - these leaders trim and tighten, and focus on the bottom line.

Soldiers like efficiency and order; they hate waste. 95% of the 'soldiers' in the study were IT or Chemistry teachers who often began their climb up the leadership ladder by managing support staff. Soldiers are tenacious when it comes to cost-cutting - often removing support staff roles - and believe those people who survive the chop need to work harder. Financial performance often improves under these leaders and does so quickly but exam results remain static and staff morale falls. As soon as the soldier leaves the school, costs simply rise back up.

3. **Accountants** - these leaders invest and grow, and focus on the top line.

3. Accountants - these leaders invest and grow, and focus on the top line.

These leaders try to grow their schools; they are resourceful, systematic and revenue-focused. 78% of the 'accountants' in the study were Maths teachers and believed schools fail because they're small and weak. These leaders are creative financiers who immediately look for new revenue sources, such as using the school's facilities for out-of-hours sports, meetings, and conferences.

Accountants improve their school's long-term financial performance and let teachers work out where to spend the extra resources. Revenue increases dramatically during these leaders' tenure, but exam results remain the same as this is not their focus. Financial performance continues improving after they leave as revenues keep growing and costs start consolidating, but exam results hardly change.

4. Philosophers - these leaders debate and discuss, and focus on values.

4. Philosophers - these leaders debate and discuss, and focus on values.

Philosophers are passionate about teaching. They're usually English or Modern Foreign Language teachers (89% in the case of the Centre for High Performance study) and believe that schools fail because they're not teaching their students properly. They think of themselves as experienced teachers, rather than as leaders.

Despite early improvements in staff morale - because colleagues feel valued and important - fundamentally, nothing really changes. Students carry on misbehaving, parents stay disengaged, and financial performance and exam results remain static.

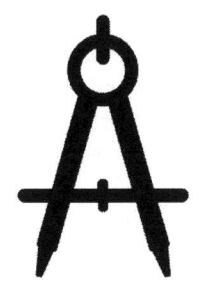

5. Architects - these leaders redesign and transform, and focus on long-term impact.

5. Architects - these leaders redesign and transform, and focus on long-term impact.

Architects quietly redesign their school and transform the community it serves. They typically studied History or Economics at university (68% of those in the study) and acquired an understanding of how past leaders created the societies and economies we live in today. They didn't set out to be teachers, but decided to initially work in industry.

Architects believe that it takes time to improve a school and so take a long-term view of what they need to do. They create the right environment for teachers and the right school for its local community. They then improve student behaviour (for example, by moving poorly behaved students into a separate pathway), increase revenue (by developing non-teaching offerings) and improve teaching and leadership (by introducing coaching, mentoring and development programmes).

In short, they take a holistic view of the school, its stakeholders, the community it serves, and its role in society. Architects are visionary, unsung heroes; stewards rather than leaders.

It will come as no surprise, reading the synopses above, that it is the architect which proves (according to the study) the most effective leader: indeed, architects are the only leaders who were found to have improved exam results over the long-term. And yet, perversely, architects are the types of leader we least reward, least recognise, and rarely appoint as principals and headteachers. Instead, we reward surgeons for dramatically increasing examination results during their tenure, even though these improvements are not sustained and tend to have a devastating impact of staff attrition. Indeed, 38% of the 68 surgeons analysed for the study had been knighted by the Queen, 24% had received a CBE, MBE or OBE, and they were paid around 50% more than the other leaders.

These are also the leaders - usually executive principals of growing academy trusts - who hog the headlines, not always for the right reasons. I've lost count of how many of the leaders celebrated by politicians and others, have later been found wanting: either because their success was short-lived and their schools have been abandoned or excised from their trusts, or because of financial irregularities or other improprieties. And why should it be this way? Because the incentive structure currently inherent in English education is much too short-termist. In short, our system honours and rewards principals and headteachers who get short-term results, no matter the means and no matter the sustainability.

Architects, who maximise impact for the maximum number of children over the maximum amount of time, meanwhile, go largely unrecognised. However, the study does offer us some hope by suggesting that schools can be made to work better with the students and teachers already working in them - a dramatic cull of staff and students might work in the short-term but is counter-productive and perhaps damaging over the long-term.

*

So far we've examined the types of leaders who have the biggest impact in turning around failing schools - not least by improving teacher recruitment and retention (of which more later). In the next chapter we will take a look at the types of organisation these great leaders build…

CHAPTER TWENTY-THREE
How kind of school is the most successful?

In a paper pithily entitled 'Organisational Blueprints for Success in High-Tech Start-Ups: Lessons from the Stanford Project on Emerging Companies' by James N. Baron and Michael T. Hannan, published in the California Management Review in 2002, the authors proposed five different models of organisational structure: the star model; the engineering model; the commitment model; the bureaucratic model; and the autocratic model.

The "star" model:
Leaders recruit from elite universities or other successful companies, and give employees huge amounts of autonomy.

Briefly, in companies which followed the "star" model, leaders recruited from elite universities or other successful companies, and gave employees huge amounts of autonomy.

The "engineering" model:
There aren't many individual stars, but engineers (the skilled craftsmen), as a group, hold the most sway.

In companies which followed the "engineering" model, there weren't many individual stars, but engineers (the skilled craftsmen), as a group, held the most sway. An engineering mindset prevailed in solving problems or approaching hiring decisions.

The "bureaucratic" model:
Cultures emerge through swollen ranks of middle leaders. Senior leaders write extensive job descriptions, organisational charts, and employee handbooks.

In the "bureaucratic" model, cultures emerged through swollen ranks of middle leaders. Senior leaders wrote extensive job descriptions, organisational charts, and employee handbooks. Everything was spelled out and everything was done by the book.

The "autocratic" model:
All the rules, job descriptions, and charts reflect the beliefs, desires and goals, not of a team, but of just one all-powerful person at the helm.

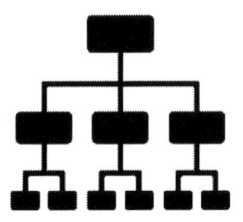

An autocratic culture, meanwhile, was similar to the bureaucratic one except that all the rules, job descriptions, and organisational charts reflected the beliefs, desires and goals, not of a senior leadership team, but of just one all-powerful person at the helm: the company was the boss.

The "commitment" model:
Focused on creating a culture in which people happily work for the same company their whole careers.

Finally, companies which followed the "commitment" model were focused on creating a culture - regarded as somewhat old-fashioned by the other organisations - in which people happily worked for the same company their whole careers. As one CEO who was interviewed for the paper put it, "I want to build the kind of company where people only leave when they retire or die."

The attitudes of the senior leaders interviewed for the paper towards organisational structure varied in three main ways: attachment; coordination/control; and selection...

In terms of 'attachment', leaders articulated three different bases of employee attachment, which the authors of the paper labelled love, work, and money.

Some leaders wanted to create a strong family-like feeling and an intense emotional bond with the workforce that would inspire superior effort and increase retention of highly sought-after employees, thereby avoiding high levels of attrition. They wanted employees to be bound to their organisation by a sense of personal belonging and identification; in other words, by a love of the company and what it did.

In terms of 'coordination and control', some leaders expressed a deep reliance on informal control through peers or organisational culture, others relied on professional control, even if they did not explicitly use this terminology. In other words, these leaders took it for granted that their employees were committed to excellence in their work and could perform at high levels because they had been professionally 'socialised' to do so. Professional control emphasised autonomy and independence, rather than enculturation. A third group of leaders took a more traditional view of control as that embedded in formal procedures and systems.

In terms of 'selection', some leaders regarded their organisation as a series of tasks and sought employees to carry out particular tasks effectively. Time and money tended to be the paramount concerns here, so the focus was on selecting employees who could be brought on-board and up-to-speed as quickly and cheaply as possible. In these cases, founders envisioned selecting employees having the skills and experience needed to accomplish some immediate tasks. Other leaders focused less on immediate and well-defined tasks than on a series of projects through which employees would move over time. Accordingly, these leaders emphasised long-term potential. Finally, a third group of leaders focused primarily on values and cultural fit, emphasising how a prospective new recruit would connect with others in the organisation.

The "engineering" organisation model involves attachment through challenging work, peer group control, and selection based on specific task abilities. In short, in "engineering" organisations, leaders will likely say: "We are very committed and the binding energy is very high."

The "star" model, meanwhile, regards attachment as being based on challenging work, a reliance on autonomy and professional control, and selecting elite personnel based on long-term potential. In short, in a "star" organisation, leaders will likely say: "We recruit only top talent, pay them top wages, and give them the resources and autonomy they need to do their job."

The "commitment" model involves a reliance on the emotional or familial ties of employees to the organisation, recruitment is based on cultural fit, and peer-group control. In short, in a "commitment" organisation, leaders will likely say: "I want to build the kind of company where people only leave when they retire."

The "bureaucracy" model involves attachment based on challenging work and/or opportunities for development, selecting individuals based on their qualifications for a particular role, and formalised control. In short, in a "bureaucratic" organisation, leaders will likely say: "Here we make sure things are documented, that people have job descriptions, and that we have rigorous project management techniques in place."

Finally, the "autocracy" model refers to employment premised on monetary motivations, control and coordination through close personal oversight, and the recruitment of employees to perform pre-specified tasks. Here, leaders will likely say: "You work, you get paid."

So which, of these five organisational models, did the researchers find to have performed best in terms of recruitment and retention, and - as a result - in relation to their productivity and effectiveness? The answer is the "commitment" model. Although the "star" model produced some of the study's most successful companies - putting all the smartest people in the same room could indeed yield vast influence and wealth - these types of organisation also failed in record numbers and rarely sustained their performance and success over the long-term.

The only culture that was a consistent winner - lasting the course and sustaining success - was the one built on commitment. In fact, "commitment" organisations outperformed every other type of organisation in almost every meaningful way.

One of the paper's authors said: "Not one of the commitment firms we studied failed. None of them, which is amazing in its own right. But they were also the fastest companies to go public, had the highest profitability ratios, and tended to be leaner, with fewer middle managers, because when you choose employees slowly, you have time to find people who excel at self-direction."

There was a sense of trust among staff and leaders that enticed everyone to work harder and stick together through the setbacks that were inevitable in any industry. Most commitment companies avoided making staff redundant unless there was no other alternative. Instead, they invested heavily in professional development.

There were higher levels of teamwork and psychological safety. Commitment companies might not have had lavish cafeterias, but they offered generous maternity leaves, childcare facilities, and flexible working options where possible. Although such initiatives were not immediately cost-effective, the commitment companies valued making employees happy over quick profits and, as a result, workers tended to turn down higher-paying jobs at rival organisations. Employees also worked smarter and better when they believed they had more decision-making authority and when they believed their colleagues were equally committed to their success.

For the commitment-model organisation, the key human resources imperative was fostering a strong culture and ensuring that new recruits fit that culture. Leaders in these organisations were more selective and devoted more effort upfront to designing their cultures and employment practices. Not surprisingly, the amount of early attention that leaders devoted to organisational concerns - such as drafting a vision and mission statement, creating an organisation chart, preparing a staff handbook, etc - was greatest in commitment organisations.

In short, then, the commitment organisations thought hard about staff recruitment - they ensured they hired the best people. Then they worked hard to ensure those staff stayed. Attrition was low because people wanted to stay, they felt valued and rewarded, and - perhaps more importantly - they felt that they were being developed professionally.

It is no coincidence that, as we discovered in the previous chapter, the most successful type of school leader - the architect - was the one which developed exactly this kind of organisation: one built on commitment. as we discovered, architects accepted that it took time to improve a school and so they took a long-term view, and they focused on creating the right environment in which teachers could thrive.

People are, after all, a school's most precious - and indeed costly - resource and so it pays to invest in them. Get recruitment right - hire the right people - and then focus on making them want to stay - thus reducing attrition and the monetary and time costs that follow, and you will develop a school that sustainably succeeds over the long-term.

*

In Smarter, Faster, Better, Charles Duhigg offers eight tips to improve organisational effectiveness - including staff recruitment and retention.

Firstly, in order to increase staff motivation, he says leaders must allow colleagues choices that put them in greater control of their roles. This might involve connecting something they do to something they care about, explaining to them why a task will help them get closer to a meaningful goal. In short, staff need to know why their work matters.

Secondly, staff need clear goals - ideally stretch goals which reflect their ambitions and aspirations. But such goals need breaking down into sub-goals and SMART objectives.

Thirdly, staff need to stay focused. This involves planning ahead, considering the order in which tasks need to be undertaken, foreseeing potential barriers.

Fourthly, staff need to be helped to make better decisions. In other words, They need to imagine various possibilities - some of which might be contradictory - so that they're better equipped to make wise choices.

Fifthly, leaders need to foster effective teams by managing the 'how' not the 'who'. In other words, leaders need to help develop staff's psychological safety by ensuring that everyone in a team feels that they can speak in roughly equal measure and that teammates show they are sensitive to how each other feels. As school leaders, we need to think about the message our decisions reveal. Are we encouraging equality in speaking, or rewarding the loudest people? Are we showing we are listening by repeating what people say and replying to questions and thoughts? Are we demonstrating sensitivity by reacting when someone seems upset or flustered? Are we showcasing that sensitivity so that other people will follow our lead?

Next, in order to improve staff's productivity, leaders need to develop lean and agile management techniques and delegate control because, as we have seen, staff work smarter and better when they believe they have more decision-making authority and when they believe their colleagues are also committed to their success. By pushing decision making to whoever is closest to a problem, we can take advantage of everyone's expertise and unlock innovation. A sense of control can also fuel motivation, but for that drive to produce insights and solutions, staff need to know that their contributions won't be ignored and that their mistakes won't be held against them.

Also, in order to encourage greater innovation, leaders need to become a broker - because creativity often emerges by combining old ideas in new ways - and encourage brokerage within their organisation. This entails being sensitive to our own experiences, paying attention to how things make us think and feel which will help us to distinguish clichés from real insights. We leaders need to study our own emotional reactions and recognise that the stress that emerges amid the creative process isn't a sign that everything is falling apart; rather, creative desperation is often critical. Anxiety can be what often pushes us to see old ideas in new ways. Finally, leaders need to remember that the relief that accompanies a creative breakthrough, while rewarding, can also blind us to alternatives. By forcing ourselves to critique what we've already done, by making ourselves look at working practices from different perspectives, by giving new authority to someone who didn't have it before, we can retain a clear perspective and oversight.

Finally, in order to improve organisational effectiveness, leaders need to help staff to understand and use data better. When we and our colleagues encounter new information, we and they should force ourselves to do something with it. For example, we should write a note explaining what we just learned, or identify a means of testing out an idea. Every choice we make in life is an experiment - the trick is getting ourselves and our colleagues to see the data embedded in those decisions, and then to use it somehow so we - and they - can learn from it.

Charles Duhigg echoes an argument espoused in the book Drive by Dan Pink. Intrinsic motivation, Pink argues, is three-fold:

1. Autonomy - the desire to direct our own lives,
2. Mastery - the urge to get better and better at something that matters,
3. Purpose - the yearning to do what we do in the service of something larger than ourselves.

Firstly, Pink says that "people need autonomy over task (what they do), time (when they do it), team (who they do it with), and technique (how they do it)". The theory behind it is as follows: if someone is in control of their activities, they are more likely to be motivated by them and more likely to excel at them.

Secondly, Pink says that "only engagement can produce mastery - becoming better at something that matters". He goes on to say that "mastery begins with 'flow' - optimal experiences when the challenges we face are exquisitely matched to our abilities - [and] requires the capacity to see your abilities not as finite, but as infinitely improvable." Again, this is about the desire to improve, to want to get better and better at something. People are only motivated to get better at something they are engaged in and enjoy. Pink goes on to say that "Mastery is a pain: it demands effort, grit and deliberate practice. And mastery is asymptote: it's impossible to fully realise, which makes it simultaneously frustrating and alluring."

And, thirdly, Pink says that humans seek purpose, "a cause greater and more enduring than themselves". This is to say that people need to feel that what they are doing will have a long-term purpose and meaning in the world. It's the desire to leave your mark on the world, to do something worthwhile and with impact.

Pink provides a useful example of the power of autonomy, mastery and purpose in action. He takes us back to 1995 and asks an economist to consider two business models, each concerned with developing a new encyclopaedia: the first model comes from Microsoft, a multi-million pound global organisation; the other is the result of a not-for-profit 'hobby'. Microsoft's encyclopaedia involves a band of paid professional writers and editors working for well-paid managers who oversee a project which is delivered on time and on budget. Microsoft sell the encyclopaedia on CD-ROMs and online. The hobbyists, meanwhile, do not belong to a company and are not paid. Instead, tens of thousands of people write and edit entries in the encyclopaedia just for fun. Contributors offer their time and expertise for nothing and the encyclopaedia itself is offered free of charge to anyone who wants it via the internet.

Clearly, any economist worth his or her salt would predict that the first business model led by Microsoft would go on to thrive whilst the second model would falter. But by 2009, Microsoft had discontinued 'Encarta' whilst 'Wikipedia' continued to thrive - with 13 million entries in 260 languages, it had become the largest and most popular encyclopaedia in the world. The business model that relied on traditional rewards to motivate its employees and customers had failed; the one that relied on intrinsic motivation (doing something simply for the fun of it) had succeeded; in the battle for supremacy, money had lost to the love of learning.

The most successful school leaders build cultures on the foundations of autonomy, mastery and purpose. And then they do something else, something just as important and just as powerful though rarely found in the pages of leadership manuals: they show kindness...

As I said at the very start of this book, the best leaders genuinely care for others and don't mind who knows it. They respect their staff's dignity, no matter their role in school. In short, the best leaders engage in small, but regular, acts of kindness towards others; the little things they do to recognise and reward their staff and students build morale and engender trust.

Kindness also plays a significant part in developing a momentum around school improvement: when people feel valued and cared for, they repay that trust by valuing and caring for the place in which they work and for the people with which they work. What's more, by publicly displaying kindness, the best leaders - and, in turn, the best teachers - model the behaviours they want their students to develop. In short, teachers who are treated with respect show respect for their students and that way a school becomes a community, a family.

I'm lucky enough, in the course of my working week, to visit a lot of schools and I've become attuned to this dynamic. In the best schools, I can sense - almost immediately upon walking through the gates - the love and care that children and adults feel towards one another. In the best schools, the staffroom remains a hub of the school - it is busy with staff sharing and listening; offloading and laughing. Conversely, in the least successful schools, the staffroom is either non-existent or deserted; instead, staff work in departmental silos or, worse, alone in their classrooms.

In the best schools, the canteen and corridors are calm, friendly places - respected and kept clean by everyone. People are polite, greeting you with a smile; and they are purposeful, focused on learning and teaching. In the least successful schools, meanwhile, there's a threatening atmosphere of chaos and confusion. There are no-go areas, behaviour isn't tackled because there is no leadership from the top: rather, behaviour is regarded as a teacher's responsibility and if they can't manage it, they alone are to blame.

In the best schools, leaders develop a 'no-blame' culture. They believe that, just because someone has made a mistake, this doesn't mean they should suddenly forget the important contribution which the same colleague makes every day. In fact, in such situations, they know that staff need to feel supported and trusted to learn from their mistake and to move on. When things are going well, meanwhile, the best leaders are generous with their praise and recognition.

No-blame cultures have proven vital to the success of organisations. In Black Box Thinking, Matthew Syed says that the most successful organisations in the world - and he uses the example of aviation - show a willingness and tenacity to investigate the lessons that often exist when we fail, but which we rarely exploit. A no-blame culture, Syed argues, is about creating systems and cultures that enable organisations to learn from errors, rather than being threatened by them.

After all, practice - which we teachers tell our students is a vital part of the learning process - is all about harnessing the benefits of learning from failure while reducing its cost. As Syed says, "It is better to fail in practice in preparation for the big stage than on the big stage itself." Or, as Eleanor Roosevelt put it, we should "learn from the mistakes of others [because we] can't live long enough to make them all [ourselves]".

Syed says the 'paradox of success' is that is it build upon failure. Everything we know in, say, aviation, every rule in the rule book, every procedure we have, we know because someone somewhere died. As Syed phrases it: "We have purchased at great cost, lessons literally bought with blood that we have to preserve as institutional knowledge and pass on to succeeding generations. We cannot have the moral failure of forgetting these lessons and have to relearn them."

And yet we can only learn from failure if there is an openness to admit to mistakes. If staff feel threatened of owning up to errors, they are less likely to do so and so that rich seam of intelligence will be lost to us, we'll keep on making the same mistakes over and over again. Only if we operate a no-blame culture will colleagues willingly admit when they get it wrong and then we can work together to get it right next time.

This is why the best teams seemingly make the most mistakes. They don't; they just admit and record them more willingly and more often. Closeted teams who fear failure and blame, don't record their mistakes and so appear, to the outside, to be more successful. This is why the world of medicine appears more infallible than the world of aviation: doctors, particularly in the US where there is a litigious culture, rarely admit to making surgical mistakes. Rather, whenever things go wrong in the operating theatre, it's about inherent risk and factors outside their control. Pilots, meanwhile, alive through testimony and dead through black boxes, openly articulate what they did wrong so that the profession can learn from it and make flying safer and safer.

Surgeons leading 'bureaucratic' or 'autocratic' schools create a closed-shop culture built on a fear of failure and a prevalence of blame. Architects leading 'committment' schools, meanwhile, build trust and openness, and thus develop autonomy, mastery and purpose. They build for the future, they develop sustainable models by investing in their people and reducing attrition.

So look to schools where staff turnover is relatively small. Fear those schools who haemorrhage staff every summer.

Talking of which, in the final chapter of this book we will take a closer look at the matter of teacher recruitment and retention…

CHAPTER TWENTY-FOUR
How can school leaders recruit and retain good teachers?

Resolving the teacher recruitment and retention crisis is proving an increasingly urgent task for school leaders in England today.

The best education systems in the world - such as the oft-cited Finland - succeed, at least in part, because they attract high quality candidates into the profession. Then they train them well - ITT being a rigorous affair which only the best survive - invest in their continued professional development throughout their careers, and reward them appropriately.

Accordingly, if our schools are to succeed, we too must ensure that we have a rich supply of qualified, high-quality teachers entering the classroom, and then we must invest in them professionally and make them feel valued in order to ensure, once they enter the profession, they remain within it. But, to be blunt, the current climate regarding recruitment and retention is dire. Before we explore some ways of resolving the crisis, let's first examine its causes...

Firstly, pupil numbers are growing. This is due to a demographic bulge which is travelling through the education system, causing a large increase in pupil numbers at secondary level. The secondary school population – not counting Year 12 and 13 pupils – is projected to rise from 2.72 million in 2017 to 3.03 million by 2021, a rise of 11.5 per cent over four years. What's more, by 2025 there's projected to be 3.3 million 11 – 15 year olds in English schools, which is an increase of half a million compared to 2015. If we are to ensure these children are properly educated, we will need an extra 26,500 teachers in the classroom.

Secondly, not enough new secondary school trainee teachers are coming into the sector. Initial Teacher Training (ITT) figures for 2016/17 show a decrease in the overall number of recruits compared with 2015/16, with only 93% of places being filled. The overall contribution to the secondary target was 89%, meaning nearly 2,000 places went unfilled. But the reality is even worse than these figures suggest because, since 2015/16, ITT figures have included applicants for Teach First who were previously excluded from these statistics. This therefore boosted the overall figure for 2016/17 by over 1,000 applicants. However, despite the inclusion of Teach First applicants in the ITT statistics, the overall Teacher Supply Model (TSM) target was still not met, just as it hadn't been met for the previous four years.

In 2016/17, the only subjects where the TSM recruitment target was met were biology, geography, history and PE. All other secondary subjects were under-recruited, and some by a significant margin. For instance, maths only recruited 84% of the required number of trainees, physics 81%, and computing just 68%. Not only are we failing to recruit enough new teachers, we're also losing too many experienced ones…

Thirdly, teachers are leaving the profession in record numbers. Over 1 in 10 teachers left the profession in 2016. Of these, an increasing proportion left the profession for other jobs rather than retiring, suggesting their working conditions rather than their age were driving them out. And the consequence of falling recruitment and retention rates? The number of unfilled teaching post vacancies is at a record high in secondary, with 23% of schools reporting an unfilled vacancy in 2017. To put this figure into some kind of perspective, in the six years between the first and second editions of this book being published, the number of schools reporting unfilled vacancies has risen by 15.9%.

The retention problem is most pronounced in multi-academy trusts which have a higher than average rate of teachers leaving the profession, compared with single-academy trusts and maintained schools. And the leaving rate is highest among teachers who teach non-EBacc subjects which might lead us to suggest that they have been incentivised to leave the profession because their subjects are no longer being taught as the school curriculum narrows, or that they have become more frustrated or disaffected at their subject receiving less priority.

A survey by the National Union of Teachers (prior to it merging with ATL and becoming the National Education Union or NEU), carried out in March 2016, found that nearly three quarters (73%) of school leaders were experiencing difficulties in recruiting teachers, with 61% saying that the situation had got worse (42%) or much worse (19%) over the last year. The greatest problem areas, according to the survey, were in maths (36% of schools leaders were struggling to recruit in this area), science (34%) and English (23%).

The crisis in teacher recruitment means that whilst schools are struggling to fill vacancies, large numbers of pupils are being taught by unqualified teachers - or at least teachers who do not have a relevant qualification in the subject they are being asked to teach. In 2016, for example, the NUT found that only 63% of physics and 75% of chemistry teachers held a relevant post A-level qualification in the subject they taught. For maths and English, these figures were 78% and 81% respectively. And falling retention rates is also costly. An analysis by the Labour Party estimated that secondary schools spent £56 million on advertising for vacant posts in 2015, an increase of 61% from 2010. But high levels of attrition among qualified teachers is not only costly in financial terms; it also has an impact on the quality of education that schools can provide... In November 2016, for example, there were 500 fewer qualified teachers in service than in the previous year. Conversely, there were 1400 more teachers in service without qualified teacher status than there had been the year before.

*

Although the government recognises there are issues, it has thus far been unable to address them adequately enough, and continues to fall short of its own recruitment targets.

What is needed at a national level is a long-term, evidence-based strategy setting out how the government will tackle challenges associated with the supply of teachers which should include improvements to the Teacher Supply Model. And whilst recruiting sufficient numbers of new teachers is clearly necessary, the government should also focus its attentions on improving teacher retention and not solely through the lens of workload. Work-life balance is clearly a problem but many teachers cite other reasons - such as stress and a lack of autonomy - for leaving the profession. Not only is improving retention rates a more cost effective way of tackling the issues of supply and demand, but having greater numbers of experienced teachers staying in the profession will naturally deepen the pool of leadership potential, supplying our next cohort of head teachers.

At a local level, meanwhile - which is to say, in schools and academy trusts - leaders need to develop staff autonomy, mastery and purpose if they are to improve recruitment and retention of high-quality teachers.

In terms of autonomy, school leaders need to better understand what motivates staff, and accept that teachers need to feel valued, rewarded, and professionally developed. In practice, school leaders might invite staff to identify a problem that exists in their department or in the wider school. Then they might be afforded the time - and resources - to solve it in their own way, perhaps during twilight INSET or in staff meeting time. It is important to end this process by implementing staff's innovations in order to make it clear that their contributions are valued.

In terms of mastery, school leaders might wish to improve their system of performance management (as I explored earlier in this book). In particular, they may wish to sharper the focus on performance improvement and personal development rather than on compliance with a set of norms. They may also want to ensure that performance feedback derives from a wide range of sources, not just from observation and not just from the line manager.

School leaders might also introduce a means by which teachers can be recognised and rewarded for their contributions beyond exam results. This means being clear and transparent about what being a high value member of staff means, having clear and transparent processes for identifying such members of staff, and ensuring that staff know that their potential has been recognised. This might mean developing a no-blame culture of openness, offering high quality feedback that allows teachers to learn from their mistakes without fear or favour.

In terms of purpose, school leaders need to understand and articulate what their school has to offer new teachers and what makes it unique. They should talk to existing staff and pupils about why it's a good place to be then communicate this clearly and frequently. They should also be clear about the school's direction of travel - about where it is headed and how it intends to get there. In terms of the mechanism of recruitment, schools need to utilise as many sources of communication as possible, not just rely on TES Jobs. They should, for example, use social media channels such as Twitter, LinkedIn and Facebook to reach out to prospective new recruits. And they should consider the recruitment cycle, pre-empting vacancies and advertising before many competitor schools. They should also develop a dedicated section of their school website for 'Work with us' which should have a range of enticing resources such as case studies and pupil voice.

Schools should also regard the recruitment of good staff as an ongoing process that takes place all year round. They should always be on the lookout for good people and keep the communication channels open at all times. Then, once they've recruited, school leaders should create clear career pathways for their staff, especially early in their careers, so that they can envisage a bright future in their school. This might involve extending mentorship opportunities beyond the traditional NQT year. It might also involve providing opportunities for teachers to affect and direct their own goals, determine their own working practices, and engage in leadership projects as a means of motivating them through autonomy and decision-making powers.

To conclude, then, if schools are to successfully stymie the crisis in staff recruitment and retention, they need to appoint, recognise and reward architects - school leaders who quietly redesign their school and transform the community it serves. They need school leaders who understand it takes time to improve a school and so take a long-term view. They need leaders who create the right environment for teachers and the right school for its local community by improving student behaviour, increasing revenue, and improving teaching and leadership. In short, they need school leaders who take a holistic view of their school, its stakeholders, the community it serves, and its role in society.

Next, they need to allow these architects to build schools based on the 'commitment' model: these schools should engender a sense of trust among staff that entices everyone to work harder and stick together through setbacks. They should invest heavily in professional development. They should value making employees happy over quick results and gift teachers more decision-making authority. They should foster a strong culture and ensure that new recruits fit that culture. In short, they should think hard about staff recruitment in order to ensure they hire the best people, then they should work hard to ensure those staff stay by making people feel valued and rewarded, and - perhaps more importantly - making sure they are developed professionally.

And, finally, these schools need to allow teachers and other staff to develop autonomy, mastery and purpose. Autonomy is important because people need control over what they do, when they do it, who they do it with, and how they do it. After all, if someone is in control of their work, they are more likely to be motivated by it and more likely to excel. Mastery is important because people need to be challenged. After all, people are only motivated to get better at something they are engaged in and enjoy. Purpose is important because people need to feel that what they are doing will have long-term meaning and a meaning in the world. People need to feel they are doing something worthwhile and impactful.

HOW TO LEAD

ABOUT THE AUTHOR

Matt Bromley is an education author and journalist with over eighteen years' experience in teaching and leadership. He is a consultant, speaker, and trainer, and a school governor.

You can find out more about him at
www.bromleyeducation.co.uk

You can follow him on Twitter
@mj_bromley

ALSO BY THE AUTHOR

The Art of Public Speaking
How to Become a School Leader
Teach
Teach 2
Making Key Stage 3 Count
How to Learn

AS EDITOR

SPaG Book (by Matilda Rose)
Outstanding Literacy (by Matilda Rose)

Published by Spark Education Books UK
Twitter: @SparkBooksUK

Published in 2018
© Matt Bromley 2018

The right of Matt Bromley to be identified as the author of this work has been asserted by him in accordance with the Copyrights, Designs and Patents Act 1988

This eBook is copyright material and must not be copied, reproduced, transferred, distributed, leased, licensed or publicly performed or used in any way except as specifically permitted in writing by the author or publishers, as allowed by the terms and conditions under which it was purchased or as strictly permitted by applicable copyright law.

ISBN-13: 978-1981361878
ISBN-10: 1981361871

Printed in Great Britain
by Amazon